# Abortion, Obtained and Denied

*Research Approaches*

Edited by

Sidney H. Newman
Mildred B. Beck
Sarah Lewit

The Population Council

The Population Council
245 Park Avenue
New York, New York 10017

Distributed for The Population Council by
Key Book Service, Inc., 425 Asylum Street,
Bridgeport, Connecticut 06610.

Standard Book Number: 0-87834-005-X
Library of Congress Catalog Card Number: 74-169597

Printed in the United States of America by Wm. F. Fell Company,
Philadelphia, Pennsylvania.

# Contents

## Section IV. SOCIOECONOMIC ASPECTS

# Introduction

Sidney H. Newman, Ph.D.* and
Mildred B. Beck, M.S.W†

THIS VOLUME of the *Proceedings of the Workshop on Abortion Obtained and Denied: Research Approaches* contains the formal papers presented at the meeting held in Bethesda, Maryland, in December 1969. The discussions of the papers are summarized here, and a section is devoted to the major research proposals that developed from the papers and discussions.

The 1969 workshop grew out of a previous one on "Abortion: A National Public and Mental Health Problem—Past, Present, and Proposed Research," held in October 1968, a summary of which was published in the December 1969 issue of the *American Journal of Public Health*.[1] A summary report of the present workshop appeared in the May 1970 *Studies in Family Planning*.[2]

Both the first and second workshops were sponsored jointly by the National Institute of Child Health and Human Development (NICHD) and the National Institute of Mental

* Behavioral Scientist Administrator, Population & Reproduction Grants Branch, Center for Population Research, National Institute of Child Health and Human Development, Bethesda, Maryland.

† Acting Chief, Office of Information, National Center for Family Planning Services, Health Services and Mental Health Administration, Bethesda, Maryland. Formerly with the Center for Epidemiologic Services, National Institute of Mental Health, Bethesda, Maryland.

Health (NIMH). Induced abortion is a significant and vexing problem, not only in the United States but in the world as a whole. Among the many facets of this complex phenomenon are population, psychological, health, social, economic, and legal problems. The NICHD, especially its Center for Population Research, is particularly interested in the antecedents and consequences of abortion, since abortion may affect population growth and has long been used by individuals as a method of fertility regulation. The possible effects of abortion on mental health, as well as the psychological-psychiatric factors, which may lead to or follow abortion, also make this subject of special interest to the NIMH.

One of the recurring themes of the first 1968 workshop was the urgent need for dependable information on the effects of abortion, obtained and denied; on the woman and her family; as well as on population growth and family planning. As a consequence, a group of experts in pertinent fields was assembled to take a searching look at the problems associated with the outcomes of abortion.

Very little is known about the outcome of abortion as well as many other facets of abortion, and a greater understanding of these problems is imperative if society is to deal intelligently with them. Consequently, the present workshop was designed to view the outcomes of abortion in a number of researchable areas where more knowledge needs to be developed. This idea led to the main objectives of the workshop, which were: (1) to review relevant background information, including research designs, methodologies, and findings; (2) select significant researchable problems for immediate investigation; and (3) suggest relevant research approaches, procedures, and instruments for future studies. In short, the stimulation and encouragement of research to increase knowledge and understanding of the outcomes of abortion was the broad goal of the workshop.

A diverse team of experts was deemed necessary to attain the objectives of the workshop, so specialists from the following fields were asked to present papers: family planning and public health; obstetrics-gynecology; psychiatry; psychology; demography; sociology; and economics. Each paper was reviewed by commentators, experts in related areas, whose function it was to lead the discussion from the vantage point of the obstetrician-gynecologist, the epidemiologist, and the biostatistician.*

The papers and the discussions in this volume on abortion have been grouped under four major headings: (1) mortality and morbidity, (2) mental health and related considerations, (3) abortion and family planning, and (4) socioeconomic aspects. Many challenging areas for research appear in the individual papers under each of these four headings, and many additional suggestions for special areas of study emerged during the course of the discussion following each paper.

The editors' copies of all papers have been reviewed and approved by each author. To conserve time, however, the editors take responsibility for condensing and rearranging the discussion, while retaining the essence and spirit of the remarks.

## NOTES

1. Beck, M. B.; Newman, S. H.; and Lewit, S., "Abortion: a national public and mental health problem—past, present, and proposed research," *American Journal of Public Health,* 59:2131–2143 (December 1969).

2. Newman, S. H.; Beck, M. B.; and Lewit, S., "Abortion, obtained and denied: research approaches," *Studies in Family Planning,* 53:1–8 (May 1970).

* Appendix B contains the list of participants, commentators, and observers.

# SECTION I
# MORTALITY AND MORBIDITY

# Somatic Consequences of Abortion

Christopher Tietze, M.D.*

ABORTION may impair a woman's health through a variety of early and late somatic complications, which may occur at the time of the abortion or soon thereafter, or which may be discovered much later, perhaps in connection with another pregnancy or with efforts to become pregnant again.[1] The frequency and severity of complications tend to increase with the duration of pregnancy and are significantly greater in abortions during the second trimester than during the first. Somatic complications may be associated with spontaneous as well as with induced abortion. However, they occur far more frequently and tend to be more severe, and more often fatal, after abortions induced by untrained persons, including the pregnant women themselves, than either after abortions performed by qualified medical practitioners under favorable circumstances, or after spontaneous abortions.

The most frequent and usually the only complication of spontaneous abortion is uterine bleeding, which is rarely profuse in the first trimester. Infection is relatively infrequent and usually mild when it occurs; and perforation of the uterus may occur during treatment.

* Associate Director, Bio-Medical Division, The Population Council, New York, New York.

In induced abortion, the bleeding is more often profuse and may result in profound shock. The extent of infection may range from mild endometritis to severe salpingitis, peritonitis, and septicemia, leading sometimes to pelvic thrombophlebitis, bacterial endotoxic shock, and/or renal failure.[2] The most lethal forms of infection are those caused by anaerobic organisms: *clostridium perfringens* (gas gangrene) and *clostridium tetani* (lockjaw).

Another potentially dangerous type of injury associated with induced abortion is perforation of the uterus, which may lead to peritonitis. Neighboring organs such as the intestines may be traumatized. The intestines or bladder may also be injured if a hypertonic solution is injected via the abdominal route. Of less immediate concern, although probably far more numerous, are injuries to the cervix.

Less common early complications of induced abortion include the following: (a) effects on the central nervous and/or renal systems of the hypertonic salt solution entering the bloodstream directly or via the peritoneal cavity; (b) air embolism,[3] and occasionally other types of embolization,[4] to the heart and pulmonary artery, and thence into the brain and other organs; and (c) misadventures of anaesthesia. Although sensitization of Rh negative women has been observed after induced abortion as early as the second month, such cases are rare and are certainly less likely to occur than if the pregnancy were carried to term, when the amount of antigens entering the material blood stream is greater than it is in early pregnancy. In abortions induced by lay abortionists, one may see renal failure resulting from the use of poisons, such as lysol, and other systemic or local effects of toxic or corrosive agents.

## *LEGAL ABORTION: MORTALITY*

Statistics on fatal complications of abortions legally performed in hospitals are relatively accurate, since only in these cases can the numerator as well as the denominator be determined with a high degree of reliability.

Mortality associated with induced abortions performed in hospitals has dropped to exceedingly low values, according to reports from several countries in eastern Europe with reliable vital statistics. Only 69 women died among almost 2.5 million women undergoing legal abortion in Czechoslovakia and Hungary during the period 1957–67, corresponding to a mortality rate of 2.8 per 100,000 such abortions.[5] The rate was 3.9 per 100,000 during the period 1957–62 and dropped to 1.7 in 1963–67.

A slightly higher rate (4.1 per 100,000) can be computed for Japan on the basis of 278 deaths attributed to legal abortion in national cause-of-death statistics and the 6,860,000 legal abortions reported in 1959–65.[6] According to Japanese public health workers, the registration of deaths due to abortion was probably more complete than the reporting of abortions by the gynecologists authorized to perform them. If the number of abortions in Japan were in fact larger than the 6,860,000 reported for the period 1959–65, then it is possible that the mortality rate from abortion in that country was at the same level as in Czechoslovakia and Hungary.

Mortality rates of 2–4 per 100,000 legal abortions compare with rates of maternal mortality, excluding abortion, of about 20 per 100,000 pregnancies in countries with good obstetric services, and 200 per 100,000 or more in many countries in the less developed regions of the world.

Mortality associated with legal abortion is substantially higher in the countries of northern Europe than in eastern Europe or in Japan: the rate was about 40 per 100,000 in Sweden and Denmark during the early 1960s, based on 21 deaths among 52,300 legal abortions.[7] The higher death rates associated with legal abortion in northern Europe may be attributed in part to the fact that a substantial proportion of the operations were performed after the third month of gestation, whereas in the countries of eastern Europe and Japan

almost all legal abortions were performed in the first trimester of pregnancy. In addition, a proportionately greater
number of the legal abortions in northern Europe were done
on medical grounds, while in eastern Europe and in Japan
the overwhelming majority of women undergoing legal
abortion were presumably in good health.

Up-to-date information on mortality associated with legal
abortion in countries with restrictive legislation is scanty,
owing to the small number performed legally and the absence
of national systems for reporting them. The fragmentary data
available suggest relatively high mortality rates, including
many deaths attributable to the disease for which the abortion
was performed. An additional reason for a higher level of
mortality may be lack of familiarity with the operative procedures and their hazards among doctors who have little opportunity to perform abortions.

## LEGAL ABORTION: MORBIDITY

Information on the frequency of nonfatal complications of
legal abortion is far less satisfactory than information on fatal
complications, because investigators are not in agreement as
to the severity of the complaints and findings they define as
complications. It might be useful, nevertheless, to cite the
rates of complications reported in Hungary for the period
1961–65.[8] During these years, among 872,000 women undergoing legal abortions, 0.13 percent experienced perforation
of the uterus, 0.4 percent had fever of gynecologic origin, and
0.6 percent hemorrhaged after the operation. One half of one
percent of the total number had to be readmitted to a hospital because of fever and 1.1 percent, because of hemorrhage.
The sum of these rates is 2.7 percent. Doubtless, there were
other serious complications, not included under any of the
five headings reported; on the other hand, some women may
have appeared under several headings. The proportion of
women who experienced any complications is not directly

available, but was probably between 2.5 and 3 percent. Somewhat lower rates of complications have been reported from Czechoslovakia[9] and somewhat higher rates from Denmark during the same period.[10]

Of the two methods most widely employed for the termination of pregnancy during the first trimester, vacuum aspiration appears to be less traumatic and to result in less loss of blood and fewer early complications than the classical dilatation and curettage.[11] In reference to abortions in the second trimester, it is impossible to make a definitive statement about hysterotomy, compared with the instillation of hypertonic salt solution, because the patterns of complications are quite different for the two methods. The waiting period between the instillation and the expulsion of the conceptus constitutes a severe emotional strain for many women.

## *ILLEGAL ABORTION*

While it is generally recognized that mortality and morbidity are higher after illegal and self-induced abortions than after abortions legally performed in hospitals, it is not possible to quantify these higher levels in a meaningful fashion. Mortality, in particular, reflects not only the skills of the persons performing or initiating the illegal operation, but also the availability and utilization of medical and hospital services, including the quality of care, if life-threatening complications develop.

It is possible and indeed likely that in sizable communities, where antisepsis is unknown or not practiced, even today, mortality after illegal abortion reaches or exceeds a level of 1,000 per 100,000 such abortions or about one-half of the maternal mortality experienced among European royal families as recently as in the nineteenth century. For most countries, taken as a whole, the risk is certainly much lower, especially if a substantial proportion of the illegal abortions are performed by qualified medical practitioners and/or if adequate hospital care is readily available. Under these circumstances, a level of mortality of 50–100 per 100,000 illegal abortions may be a high estimate.

## CAUSE-OF-DEATH STATISTICS

While most deaths attributed to abortion are probably due to abortions induced by untrained persons, including self-induced abortions, which may or may not be illegal, it is not possible to estimate the number of such abortions from the number of deaths. During the early 1960s, the annual rate of mortality from abortion, as reported in national cause-of-death statistics, ranged from less than 1.0 per 100,000 women, 15 to 44 years of age, in most of the developed countries, to more than 10 per 100,000 in Chile. A special study sponsored by the Pan-American Health Organization revealed rates higher than 10 per 100,000 in three out of ten cities in Latin America.[12] For most of Asia and Africa, only fragmentary information is available. The geographic pattern of mortality rates appears to reflect the completeness and correctness of cause-of-death registration and the general level of health services in each country, at least as much as the number of illegal abortions and the level of skill of the persons inducing or performing them.

It is generally assumed that some deaths due to abortion are reported under other diagnoses, either unknowingly, because a correct diagnosis was not made, or intentionally. It is not possible to determine the magnitude of this error for any country. In the United States estimates of 5,000 to 10,000 deaths from abortion annually, still quoted by respectable authorities,[13] may have been reasonable when they were first published more than thirty years ago,[14] but no longer are at a time when the total number of deaths among women of reproductive age, 15 to 44 years of age from *all* causes is not more than about 50,000 annually.

According to official statistics, the number of reported

deaths from abortion in 1966 was 189 for the entire United States.[15] In my estimation, the true total of deaths due to illegal abortion, recorded and hidden, cannot have been much larger than twice the reported number, or about 400 deaths from illegal abortions per year. This estimate is based on the consideration that most women dying from the complications of an illegal abortion are likely to be admitted to a hospital and that most of them are poor and friendless and have been "helped" by lay persons, not by doctors, which should minimize the need for "covering up" by the hospital staff.

The trend in reported mortality from abortion, computed for 100,000 women 15 to 44 years of age, has been consistently downward over the past third of a century, from about 9 per 100,000 per year in the early 1930s to 0.9 in 1950 and 0.5 in 1966. This downward trend has roughly paralleled the decline in maternal mortality, *excluding* abortion, per 100,000 live births over the same period. These parallel declines are thought to reflect the remarkable progress in the treatment of puerperal infection and other complications of pregnancy, abortion, and childbirth.

Mortality from abortion remains much higher among nonwhite women than among white women, and the differential has increased substantially over the past three decades. In 1933, the mortality rate from abortion was twice as high among nonwhite women as among white women; in 1966, it was six times as high. Although the mortality rate decreased for both groups, the decline was much faster for whites than for nonwhites. The higher mortality rates for nonwhite women result, at least to a considerable extent, from the poorer quality of abortionists and of aftercare available to nonwhite women. It is by no means an indication that nonwhite women resort to abortion more often than white women.

In 1933, reported deaths from abortion accounted for 2.4 percent of all deaths among women of reproductive age; by 1966, the proportion had declined to 0.4 percent. In terms of mortality, illegal abortion is no longer a major public health problem in the United States. Its primary impact is now in terms of health, rather than life, and of human dignity, which cannot easily be quantified.

In the 1930s, the reported deaths from abortion accounted for about one-fourth of all deaths from complications of pregnancy, childbirth, and the puerperium. In the late 1940s and early 1950s, the share of abortion dropped to about one-eighth, after which it increased again, reaching one-fifth of all maternal deaths in the 1960s. These variations present a mirror image of the trend in the national birth rates.

## SOMATIC SEQUELAE

The pattern of somatic sequelae of abortion is dominated by the late manifestations of infection, including the chronic forms of pelvic inflammatory disease, peritoneal adhesions, ectopic pregnancy, and secondary sterility. Infection occurs far more frequently in association with illegal or self-induced abortion than with legal termination of pregnancy or with spontaneous abortion. The same is true for the aftermath of infection. The overall incidence of these complications has not been satisfactorily determined for any population but there is no doubt that a great amount of human suffering is involved.

By way of contrast, termination of pregnancy, competently performed, rarely produced sequelae that seriously impaired the woman's physical well-being.[16] Disturbances of menstrution are usually of limited duration.[17] Occasionally, amenorrhea may be caused by intrauterine synechiae, which may persist if untreated.[18] An increased tendency to ectopic pregnancy,[19] placenta praevia, and premature separation of the placenta has been postulated but has not been established as a sequel of legal abortion.[20] Endometriosis may develop in scar tissue following hysterotomy.[21] The condition known as incompetent cervix is frequently preceded by injuries to the cervical canal, which may occur during the performance of legal abortion as well as in other circumstances.[22]

A number of possible sequelae are associated with the reproductive function. Secondary sterility may occur, but whether it occurs more frequently after legal abortion than after delivery is not known.[23] Nor has it been established whether a woman who has had several induced abortions is more likely to become sterile after her last abortion than a woman in the same age group who has had only one induced abortion.

Studies in Hungary and in Japan have shown that premature births tend to occur more frequently among women who have had induced abortions than among women who have not had them.[24] This appears to be true regardless of age, parity, employment, and other characteristics of the mother. The frequency of prematurity tends to increase with the number of prior induced abortions.

Even the small risk to life associated with the artificial termination of pregnancy under the most favorable circumstances can be avoided by the successful practice of a safe method of contraception. Unfortunately, the most effective methods of contraception are not entirely safe; i.e., free of possible fatal complications. At least under the conditions of mortality prevailing in developed countries, the known risk to life due to thromboembolic diseases resulting from the use of currently available oral contraceptives over a given period of time is estimated to be on the same order of magnitude as the risk incurred by preventing births exclusively by abortions in hospital, not making any contraceptive efforts, over the same period. The risk to life associated with the insertion and wearing of intrauterine devices, due to pelvic inflammatory disease, and, occasionally, to perforation of the uterus resulting in intestinal obstruction, is less, but not entirely negligible.

The risk to life, associated with the prevention of unwanted births, is minimized by the use of methods of contraception that are entirely free from fatal side effects, although less than 100 percent effective, combined with the termination, in hospital, of those pregnancies that occur either through failure of the method or through improper or inconsistent use of the method.[25]

## RESEARCH NEEDS

The following is a listing of major research needs in the area of somatic consequences of abortion:

1. Evaluation of early complications associated with abortion in hospital, with special emphasis on period of gestation, technique of abortion, and type of anesthesia. While some information on these subjects is available, it is not nearly as comprehensive as one would wish, nor are data from all countries equally credible to all persons. Accordingly, cooperative statistical studies of the experience of selected ob/gyn departments of high reputation in the United States and/or the United Kingdom should have high priority. It is believed that the number of such departments at which many abortions are performed is now large enough to permit the collection of significant statistics over a period of two or three years.

2. Evaluation of early complications, associated with abortion as an outpatient procedure. Since the availability of hospital beds is likely to be a major factor limiting the utilization of abortion, it appears most urgent to determine the relative safety of the operation performed on ambulatory patients, followed by a few hours of bed rest. Ideally, stationary and ambulatory treatment should be assigned at random to eligible women aborted by the same surgeon, but it is not likely that a study of this type, involving sizeable numbers of women, can be organized. The next best approach would be to study a large series of women, nonrandomly assigned to ambulatory treatment, with systematic follow-up, which must not interfere with the routine character of the

treatment. Opportunities for investigations of this type may arise in the near future in one or more metropolitan communities in the United States.

3. Evaluation of early complications associated with abortion as a stationary or ambulatory procedure in developing countries. Several of these countries have recently liberalized their abortion policies; others may do so in the future. Substantial numbers of abortions will probably be performed in some large hospitals. Encouragement and support should be given to the collection, evaluation, and early publication of the experience thus obtained, perhaps most suitably on a grant basis.

4. Establishment of a central file of case histories involving death associated with legal abortion. Mortality has become so low as to make comparative statistics by procedure almost meaningless. This fact increases the importance of evaluating the complete history of each case that occurs and, hence, of a central file and speedy publication. The cooperation of WHO and/or FIGO might be sought for this project.

5. Evaluation of the somatic sequelae of abortions performed by qualified medical practitioners. No major study of this type appears to have been undertaken since Lindahl's work in Sweden, published in 1959, which moreover is primarily concerned with the aftereffects of hysterotomy in the second trimester. A comparable assessment of other procedures, with special emphasis on those used during the first trimester, would furnish valuable information. Studies of this type would have to be located in an environment that permits follow-up several years after the operation, including follow-up of women aborted, prior to family formation or at an early stage of family building, who may be expected to desire pregnancy at a later time. Consideration should be given to the parallel investigation of a comparable series of women who gave birth instead of aborting. Northern Europe would seem to be the most suitable site for this type of study.

6. Evaluation of the psychological sequelae of abortions

performed by qualified medical practitioners. While a rigid appraisal of this problem is not feasible owing to the impossibility of separating the effect of the procedure from the effects of selection associated with (a) request for abortion and (b) approval, a new follow-up study comparable to Ekblad's in the early 1950s might produce reassuring results.

7. Development of prognostic procedures to identify women who are likely to experience serious emotional upset subsequent to abortion. Such individuals might be counselled against having the abortion or offered supportive psychiatric treatment. This type of study might begin with an exploration in depth of a limited number of subjects who had, in fact, developed clinical symptoms. On the basis of these observations a battery of psychological tests would be designed and administered to a large number of women requesting abortion, and the predictive value of the tests verified by follow-up.

## NOTES

1. Af Geijerstam, G. K. (ed.), *An Annotated Bibliography of Induced Abortion* (Ann Arbor: Center for Population Planning, University of Michigan, 1969), pp. vi, 359.

2. Schwarz, R. H., *Septic Abortion* (Philadelphia: Lippincott, 1968), pp. xiv, 153.

3. Silver, M. D., and Evans, T. N., "Air embolism: a discussion of maternal mortality with a report of 1 survivor," *Obstetrics and Gynecology*, 31:403–405 (March 1968).

4. Goldstein, P. J., "Amniotic fluid embolism complicating intrauterine saline abortion," *American Journal of Obstetrics and Gynecology*, 101:858–859 (July 15, 1968).

5. Tietze, C., "Abortion laws and abortion practices in Europe," *Advances in Planned Parenthood* (ed. A. J. Sobrero, C. McKee), 5:194–212 (Amsterdam: Excerpta Medica International Congress Series No. 207, 1970).

6. Tietze, C., "Induced abortion as a method of fertility control," *Fertility and Family Planning* (ed. S. J. Behrman, L. Corsa, R. Freedman) (Ann Arbor: University of Michigan Press, 1969), pp. 311–337.

7. Tietze, "Abortion laws and practices in Europe," pp. 194–212.

8. Hirschler, I., Material presented at Session on Abortion and Mortality: Medical Risks Inherent in Abortions Aseptically Performed. *Abortion in a Changing World, Volume 2* (ed. Robert E. Hall) (New York: Columbia University Press, 1970), pp. 128–131.

9. Tietze, "Abortion laws and practices in Europe," pp. 194–212.

10. Olsen, C. E.; Nielsen, H. B.; Ostergaard, E., "Abortus provocatus legalis: en analyse af 21,730 anneldelser til sundhedsstyrelsen 1961–1965," *Ugeskrift for Laeger,* 129:1341–1351 (October 12, 1967).

11. Kerslake, D., and Casey, D., "Abortion induced by means of the uterine aspiration," *Obstetrics and Gynecology,* 30:35–45 (July 1967); Vojta, M., "A critical view of vacuum aspiration: a new method for the termination of pregnancy," *Obstetrics and Gynecology,* 30:28–34 (July 1967).

12. Puffer, R. R., and Griffith, G. W., *Patterns of Urban Mortality: Report of the Inter-American Investigation of Mortality* (Washington, D.C.: Pan American Health Organization, September 1967), pp. 169–181.

13. Kummer, J. M. (ed.), *Abortion: Legal and Illegal: a Dialogue Between Attorneys and Psychiatrists* (Santa Monica: Jerome M. Kummer, 1967), pp. xi, 63.

14. Taussig, F. J., *Abortion: Spontaneous and Induced* (St. Louis: Mosby, 1936), p. 28.

15. U.S. Department of Health, Education, and Welfare, Public Health Service, National Center for Health Statistics, *Vital Statistics of the United States, 1966, Volume II, Part A* (Washington, D.C.: U.S. Government Printing Office), Tables 1-13, p. 35.

16. Lindahl, J. M., *Somatic Complications Following Legal Abortion* (Stockholm: Svenska bokforlaget, 1959), pp. 182; Family Planning Federation of Japan: Sub-committee on the Study of Induced Abortion, *Harmful Effects of Induced Abortion: Reports of Studies Conducted by the* . . . (Tokyo: 1966), pp. 97.

17. Kubo, H., and Ogino, H., "Artificial abortion—current aspect and postoperative follow-up study," *Harmful Effects of Induced Abortion* (Tokyo: Family Planning Federation of Japan: Sub-committee on the Study of Induced Abortion 1966), pp. 11–26; Matsumoto, S., and Ozawa, M., "Artificial termination of pregnancy and menstrual abnormality," *Harmful Effects of Induced Abortion* (Tokyo: Family Planning Federation of Japan: Sub-committee on the Study of Induced Abortion, 1966), pp. 27–35.

18. Momose, K., "Intrauterine adhesions as seen with hysterosalpingography in relation to the intra-uterine instrumentation with pregnancy," *Harmful Effects of Induced Abortion* (Tokyo: Family Planning Federation of Japan: Sub-committee on the Study of Induced Abortion, 1966), pp. 44–48.

19. Sawazaki, C., and Tanaka, S., "The relationship between artificial abortion and extrauterine pregnancy," *Harmful Effects of Induced Abortion* (Tokyo: Family Planning Federation of Japan: Sub-committee on the Study of Induced Abortion, 1966), pp. 49–63.

20. Furusawa, Y., and Koya, T., "The influence of artificial abortion on delivery," *Harmful Effects of Induced Abortion* (Tokyo: Family Planning, 1966), pp. 74–83.

21. Brosset, A., "Endometriosis in the vaginal scar following vaginal hysterotomy for therapeutic abortion," *Acta Obstetricia et Gynecologica Scandinavica*, 33:445–456 (1954); Gottlieb, T., "Endometriosis in the vaginal scar following hysterotomy for therapeutic abortion: report on 100 cases," *Acta Obstetricia et Gynecologica Scandinavica*, 36:194–208 (1957).

22. Forster, F. M. C., "Abortion and the incompetent cervix," *Medical Journal of Australia*, 2:807–809 (October 28, 1967).

23. Hayashi, M., and Momose, K., "Statistical observation on artificial abortion and secondary sterility," *Harmful Effects of Induced Abortion* (Tokyo: Family Planning Federation of Japan: Sub-committee on the Study of Induced Abortion, 1966), pp. 36–43.

24. Barsy, G., and Sarkany, J., "A müvi vetélések hatása a születési mozgalomra és a csecsemöhalarndósagra," *Demográfia*, 4:427-267 (1963); Miltényi, K., "A müvi vetélések hatásainak kérdésehez," *Demográfia*, 7:73-87 (1964); Moriyama, Y., and Hirokawa, O., "The relationship between artificial termination of pregnancy and abortion or premature birth," *Harmful Effects of Induced Abortion* (Tokyo: Family Planning Federation of Japan: Sub-committee on the Study of Induced Abortion, 1966), pp. 64–73.

25. Tietze, C., "Mortality with contraception and induced abortion," *Studies in Family Planning*, 45:6–8 (September 1969).

# Outcomes of Induced Abortion: Medical-Clinical View

Irvin M. Cushner, M.D.*

THIS PAPER discusses from the medical-clinical view the various consequences which befall women whose pregnancies are terminated before the fetus is viable. My presentation will be from the vantage point of the "performer."

In the current patterns of availability of abortion services in the United States, one of the following four persons may interrupt a pregnancy: (1) the gynecologist in a hospital, (2) the gynecologist outside a hospital, (3) the nongynecologist-physician outside a hospital, (4) the nonphysician outside a hospital, including the patient herself.

Except for the very recent and unique situation in the District of Columbia, where, for all intents and purposes, no law regarding abortion exists at this time, one will quickly recognize that it is only the first of these "performers" who is operating openly and within the framework of legality, whose observations and data are available, and who works in an atmosphere which engenders a minimal risk of complication. At the same time, it is also clear that because of his well-known conservative stance, the first performer does a small

* Associate Professor of Gynecology and Obstetrics; Director, Center for Social Studies in Human Reproduction, The Johns Hopkins University School of Medicine, Baltimore, Maryland.

minority of the induced abortions in this country. Elsewhere, his three out-of-hospital counterparts do the overwhelming majority, but their observations and data are generally unavailable, and the risk of complication is inversely related to their skill and experience as well as to their utilization of available medical and hospital resources.

At first glance, one might assume that the only way to reduce the risk of complication is through a program that brings all women desirous of abortion to the hospital gynecologist and that eliminates the need for all other types of providers of this service. However, this is not necessarily the case. Indeed, if tomorrow the U. S. Supreme Court were to declare all laws restricting abortion null and void, if every woman in the United States desiring an abortion would then seek it from a hospital-based gynecologist, and if the termination of pregnancy remained a surgical procedure, it is perfectly clear that there would be a serious deficiency in the numbers of willing gynecologists, of operating and delivery suites, and of hospital beds. In addition, a significant number of women would be unable to pay the current medical and hospital charges for abortion and/or unwilling to reveal their unwanted pregnancy to a welcoming committee of hostile personnel or to the community.

The decisions, which will have to be made by society in general and by the health care industry specifically, will revolve around the development of new styles, new systems, and new types of settings and personnel for the delivery of abortion services. However, it will be essential—indeed, demanded—that any innovations in care be based on documented evidence that the risk of complication does not exceed the minimal risk now assumed for the traditional mode of the gynecologist operating in a hospital. The need for research into somatic outcomes, then, takes on this very important dimension—that the findings will represent the basis upon which proposed programs can be planned and implemented.

In order to determine these research needs, it will be necessary first to review the medical-clinical aspects of mortality and morbidity from induced abortion. We must examine those issues that face the individual physician and the individual patient as they evaluate the need for an induced abortion, plan for its performance, and identify how some of these issues affect the risk of complication.

## MORTALITY AND MORBIDITY

WHAT ARE THE "KNOWNS" REGARDING COMPLICATIONS?

Based upon data available from records of hospital admissions for the complications of induced abortion, as well as records of complications which occur following hospital-performed abortions, the statements below can be made with a high degree of accuracy. The risks of complications associated with induced abortion are: (1) lowest in abortions performed in hospitals by gynecologists and highest in abortions performed outside of hospitals by nonphysicians or by the woman, herself, (2) higher in the nonwhite population than in the white population, (3) higher after the twelfth week of gestation than earlier in pregnancy, (4) higher if a medical-surgical contraindication exists at the time of the operation.

In the last two years, the number of complications in out-of-hospital abortions seems to be declining. This observation was reinforced by the testimony given by Dr. Milton Halpern, Chief Medical Examiner of New York City, before the Joint Committee of the New York Legislature, which was considering a revision of that state's abortion law in 1969.* Dr. Halpern stated that, during his long tenure as medical examiner, he had observed a progressive decline in the number of deaths associated with criminal abortion, but that the numbers still remained unacceptably high. What was more

* New York State has since enacted a law, which went into effect July 1, 1970, providing for the termination of pregnancy through the 24th week of gestation if the woman and her physician agree.

significant in his testimony was his comment that the specific causes of deaths also appeared to be changing. According to his analysis, this change was probably due to the fact that more abortions were being performed by qualified physicians and that, therefore, the patient was obtaining not only additional skill in performance but the additional ingredients of good postoperative care, unavailable to her from the non-physician abortionist (e.g., antibiotic drugs, oxytocic drugs, etc.).

Furthermore, it is of some interest to note that in Maryland, during the first year of the new abortion law, there were no deaths reported among 2,142 hospital-performed abortions. At The Johns Hopkins Hospital, there were no deaths reported among 1,178 hospital-performed abortions. Three deaths were reportedly due to complications of abortion performed outside of hospitals.

WHAT ARE THE SOCIAL AND CLINICAL FACTORS
AFFECTING THE RISK OF COMPLICATION AND
WHAT IS THEIR INTERRELATIONSHIP?

(1) *Duration of Pregnancy*

The clinical issue here is based on the facts that the more advanced the pregnancy, the more tissue must be removed, the greater is the vascularity of the uterus, the larger is the placental bed, the greater is the risk of perforation and of retained products, and the longer is the procedural time.

There are two social issues: (a) a marked tendency to delay the reporting of the pregnancy and, thus, the receipt of pre-natal care among the very young, the unmarried, the non-white, and the poor; and (b) procedural delays imposed by socio-administrative imperatives, such as the presumed need for psychiatric consultation, the need for hospital adminis-trative approval, the limited availability of hospital beds and of operating room time.

The interrelationship between the socio-administrative and clinical factors is therefore associated with the reluctance of certain groups to make their pregnancies known, and the superimposed procedural delays brought about by the provisions of the present state law and hospital requirements, which together lead to a longer duration of pregnancy at the time the woman is admitted for the operative termination. Witness the fact that among 1,178 abortions performed at The Johns Hopkins Hospital during the first year of the new law, 45 percent were performed by vacuum aspiration and/or dilatation and curettage (D & C); 45 per cent, by saline injection; and 10 percent, by abdominal laparotomy (either hysterotomy and tubal sterilization or hysterectomy). Since the operative procedure selected is determined almost exclusively by the duration of the pregnancy, these data suggest that almost half of our patients were victims of social, administrative, and medical delays.

(2) *Operative Procedure*

As noted above, the operative procedure is determined primarily by the duration of the pregnancy. In general, pregnancies of less than twelve weeks' duration are terminated by vacuum aspiration or the traditional curettage. Those of longer duration can be terminated by the intra-amniotic injection of hypertonic saline which, within twelve to thirty-six hours, usually induces uterine hypermotility, with subsequent cervical dilation and the rupture of the membranes eventuating in uterine evacuation. In the institutions using this procedure, saline injections have, for all intents and purposes, replaced abdominal hysterotomy, which was formerly the only procedure available after twelve weeks' gestation. Under these circumstances, the abdominal procedures are now being used almost exclusively for patients who also need concomitant sterilization. The procedure can therefore be either hysterotomy with a tubal sterilization, or, where indicated, hysterectomy.

In early pregnancy terminations, the vacuum aspiration technique is becoming more popular and more widely used than the traditional D & C. In those institutions which have the apparatus and have learned its value, it has become quite clear that the advantages are a markedly shortened operating time, significantly reduced blood loss, and less cervical dilation in the primigravida. The last-mentioned advantage should go a long way toward preventing cervical lacerations and the cervical incompetence that can follow the excessive dilation needed to insert the instruments used in the traditional D & C.

In terminations later in pregnancy, the induction of abortion by saline injection has the obvious advantage over abdominal procedures because it avoids a major surgical operation; i.e., laparotomy. However, the patient's experiences are not nearly as acceptable or innocuous as in early termination. Saline injections cannot be safely used until the sixteenth week of pregnancy, thereby necessitating a further delay if the patient is not admitted by the twelfth-week deadline required for the simpler method. In addition, the actual termination is a form of labor associated with some discomfort, which can be intensified by any underlying psychologic factors, as well as those which are superimposed by the delay necessitated by waiting until the sixteenth week of pregnancy. Finally, there is always the risk that if the sedation is inadequate, the patient will be awake when the fetus is expelled. All of this may contribute to a higher risk of adverse psychological sequelae than if the termination occurred early in pregnancy when the operative procedures used are faster and less unpleasant.

The clinical issues related to the risk of complication are inherent in the fact that the specific causes of mortality and morbidity are surgical complications arising largely from the abortion procedure itself, namely, hemorrhage, infection, uterine perforation. In other words, the risk exists specifically because, at this time in history, the artificial termination of pregnancy is a surgical rather than, for example, a pharmacological one. It is, therefore, justifiable to anticipate that these risks exist regardless of whether the procedure is carried out by the professor of obstetrics in the university medical center or by the nonphysician abortionist in a clandestine environment. It has been assumed that only the degree of risk is variable, and that it is related, not to the medical procedure, but to the skill of the operator and the readiness of his facility to respond to unanticipated emergency complications. This, however, is not borne out by the data provided in the first annual report for the state of Maryland on the abortion practices and experiences in that state during the first year of its new law.

As an index of the risk of complication, each Maryland hospital is required to include in its annual reports data on the incidence of "morbidity," defined as a fever of 100.4°F. on any two days, exclusive of the first twenty-four hours. While these data are not specific for the incidence of hemorrhage, infection, and uterine perforation, they can be accepted as a gross index, since these complications would certainly contribute to the morbidity as defined. The morbidity data for the state of Maryland and for The Johns Hopkins Hospital are as follows:

|  | Maryland | | Johns Hopkins Hospital | |
|---|---|---|---|---|
|  | Number | Percent | Number | Percent |
| Vacuum aspiration | 2/435 | 0.5 | 0/358 | 0.0 |
| D & C | 12/580 | 2.1 | 0/83 | 0.0 |
| Saline injection | 25/888 | 2.8 | 14/617 | 2.3 |
| Hysterotomy and hysterectomy | 52/239 | 21.8 | 36/120 | 30.0 |

The social issues relating operative procedures to complications would, of course, be similar to the social issues mentioned earlier regarding duration of pregnancy. The same problems of late reporting plus procedural delays bring the patients to the operating room more frequently than we like for procedures which carry with them higher risks of complications even in the best of hands and in the best of facilities.

The interrelationship between the social and the clinical in this area brings into focus an increased risk of complication and a greater "medical commitment" in terms of longer hospital stay, greater cost, and longer time away from work or school, because of the socially influenced factors of late pregnancy reporting and procedural delays.

It might be well to reemphasize at this point that the data noted above represent morbidity, not mortality. There were no deaths from hospital abortions and one must not lose sight of the fact that even the data on morbidity indicate a relatively low risk of complication among pregnancies terminated vaginally.

### (3) Postoperative care

Adequate postoperative care plays a preventive role in complications from induced abortion by affording their earlier detection as well as their earlier and more adequate treatment. Three aspects of postoperative care must be well understood in order to appreciate the needs in this area.

The time of onset of the various complications varies somewhat. Most cases of serious hemorrhage occur within the first twelve to twenty-four hours. The first signs of infection appear within the first forty-eight to seventy-two hours. The evidence of uterine perforation might be immediate or it might develop more insidiously over the first twelve to twenty-four hours. The occasional cases of biochemical abnormalities associated with saline injection usually reveal themselves in the first several hours after the injection.

The minimal observations necessary for early detection also vary according to the complications. In cases of hemorrhage, the acute dramatic hemorrhage, which immediately follows the procedure, is quite obvious. On the other hand, the more insidious type of excessive bleeding can be detected only by the kind of observations made in an intensive care-type unit or, at the minimum, in a situation where at least the perineal pads are saved and counted. In the case of infection, the minimal observations required would be regular determination of temperature and frequent observation for abdominal distension, tenderness, or rigidity. Uterine perforation can be detected early only if the patient is being carefully observed for signs of internal bleeding, fever, and abdominal distension. The clinical clues associated with biochemical abnormalities following saline injection include severe thirst, severe headache, tachycardia, and hypotension.

Knowledgeability and available facilities for adequate treatment are of utmost importance. In cases of hemorrhage, this includes the contemporary treatment of shock, as well as the use of blood and blood substitutes. In cases of infection, the essential features are the use of very large doses of antibiotic drugs, supported by laboratory studies, knowledge of available antibiotics for sensitive and refractory patients, and sophisticated intensive treatment resources in cases of endotoxic shock. For uterine perforation, the obvious need is an immediately available operating room for laparotomy and the surgical wisdom required in the decision to either repair the laceration or perform hysterectomy.

What has been described above would, therefore, represent the purely clinical issues. The social issues have to do with the variable availability of minimum standards of postoperative care in out-of-hospital abortions, or, in some cases, even in hospitals in which abortions are done so rarely that the staff and the hospital are unprepared. The most serious social problems, however, are seen in those cases in which women must choose an out-of-hospital facility because of restrictive laws and an unwilling medical profession, or because of the high costs, which they cannot afford to pay.

There is an interesting interrelationship between the social and the clinical in this area. It has been mentioned earlier that there is reasonable evidence that the numbers of abortion deaths and admissions for complications seem to be declining as a result of an increase in out-of-hospital abortions performed by physicians with the concomitant advantages which accrue from their knowledge and training, as compared to those of nonphysician abortionists. It would, therefore, be reasonable to assume that even the patient who must choose an out-of-hospital abortion can minimize her risk of complication if she is able to obtain the services of a competent physician, albeit, in his nonhospital clandestine facility.

## RESEARCH NEEDS

### AIMS

In discussing the goals of research needed to reduce to a minimum the risk of complication from induced abortion, it is necessary to reiterate and reemphasize some of the points already made. It must be remembered that mortality and morbidity are already negligible in hospital-performed abortions and that they are declining even in the out-of-hospital procedures for reasons already mentioned. It is, therefore, necessary to maintain the high standards of care implicit in this trend; namely, that the risk of complication is minimized by the technical proficiency and medical knowledgeability of the operator and by the accessibility and adequacy of the facility to detect and deal with possible emergency situations. At the same time, it is very clear, again, that if all women in this country who want and need an induced abortion were to present themselves to hospitals, their numbers would overwhelm the bed capacities of the hospitals and the physical capacities of the available and willing personnel. Finally, the risks are enhanced by the surgical nature of the procedure, by the reluctance of women to report early and reveal their pregnancy, and by the inability of many patients to afford the cost of this care.

Therefore, research in these areas should be aimed at the development of improved methods and improved systems of service which have the following features: (1) minimal delay, (2) minimal risk of immediate and longer-term complications, (3) low cost, (4) determination of any propensity or vulnerability to complication, and (5) competent personnel who are nonjudgmental and compassionate.

IMPROVED METHODS

The following questions need be answered regarding projected methodology in the artificial termination of human pregnancy:

(1) Can a method be developed to terminate an unwanted or high-risk pregnancy in its extremely early stages by a physician in his office or in an outpatient facility? Is this possible with such measures as electrostimulation or, perhaps, cryosurgery, within the uterine cavity, using an intrauterine probe small enough to be inserted without cervical dilation? It might be feasible to initiate the process at such an early stage with such procedures.

(2) Can the methodology in saline amniocentesis be improved to shorten the latent phase between injection of the saline solution and the onset of abortion, and to reduce the incidence of retained secundines? In a study of the experience with this procedure at The Johns Hopkins Hospital, which is not yet completed, the data so far suggest that while the complication rate was extremely low, the two problems of significant magnitude were retained placental fragments and some cases of unduly long latent periods. The data further suggest the possibility that measures, such as slight overdistension of the uterus by injecting more saline than the volume of amniotic fluid withdrawn, plus the earlier use of oxytocin stimulation, might be valuable ameliorative procedures.

(3) Is it feasible to develop an orally effective, safe, abortifacient drug? One group of drugs with promise are the luteolytic agents which, if taken either postcoitally or during the postovulatory phase of the cycle, would prevent luteal function, thereby preventing implantation or maintenance of the already implanted zygote. Some rather encouraging reports have been published regarding the use of prostaglandin for induction of labor as well as for the termination of first

and second trimester pregnancies. The initial reports indicate high rates of success with intravenous infusions. Subsequently, work has included the intra-muscular subcutaneous oral and vaginal (suppository) routes, with varying degrees of success. Further clinical studies will be needed to definitively determine prostaglandin's effectiveness and hazards. Antizygotic drugs have also been considered but with the inherent fear that failure (that is, failure to abort) would be associated with teratogenesis. Needless to say, the conversion of induced abortion from a surgical procedure to a pharmacologically induced experience would add immeasurably to the reduction of some of the complications of contemporary methods.

SYSTEMS OF SERVICE

(1) Can a community be influenced to respond to the advantages of early pregnancy reporting and detection? It is necessary to develop methods of community education and orientation regarding the availability of abortion, its role in contraceptive failures and other unwanted pregnancies, and the significantly reduced risks when the procedure is done very early in pregnancy. The fact that cost is appreciably reduced at the same time should be further inducement to early reporting.

It is also necessary to document the advisability of providing community programs and resources for free and confidential pregnancy detection. Such a community-based facility should ultimately attract patients very early in pregnancy for performance of the urinary assay technique, which can be done cheaply and can be competently performed by nonmedical, community personnel. Correlation in such a center of the presence or absence of pregnancy with its desirability or undesirability will then afford the possibility of referral of women for whichever services are needed: prenatal care, adoption or foster care services, abortion, sterility-infertility studies, or better methods of family planning. It will be necessary to determine the motivational and attitudinal factors involved in pregnancy reporting, as well as in the persons and facilities where the detection and counseling will be done.

(2) Is it possible to document the safety of induced abortion as outpatient procedures in hospitals? This would, of course, reduce the cost considerably and would also free hospital beds otherwise occupied by such patients. A preliminary effort in this direction at The Johns Hopkins Hospital (about 100 patients to date) corroborates the vast experience in the eastern European countries and elsewhere; namely, that vacuum aspiration performed at less than ten weeks of pregnancy is safe when there is optimal postoperative observation. Very few patients have required postoperative admissions and no patients have required postdischarge readmissions. An additional safeguard would be the development of postdischarge follow-up by home visits.

A further system change, which will have to be evaluated for safety, is the possibility that vacuum aspiration could be safely performed, if done earlier in pregnancy (less than nine weeks) in licensed, outpatient facilities or licensed, small hospitals, located close to a general hospital. There is already some experience being gained in such facilities in England. The basic requirements for safety in such a facility would include the ready availability of blood, anesthesia, resuscitation personnel and equipment, and adequate facilities for postoperative observation and follow-up.

The combination of safe, outpatient procedures used in hospitals and safe procedures used in facilities near hospitals would go a long way toward the solution of the problem of available beds and operating rooms, if increasingly large numbers of patients should choose to request this service from the health care industry (to which they will be entitled if abortion laws cease to exist).

(3) Can the education and training of personnel be improved so as to provide to society larger numbers of competent operators and competent advisors who are able to render non-

judgmental service? It will be necessary to examine the knowledge and attitudes of medical students, residents, nurses, and
social workers in the areas associated with population, human
sexuality, fertility control, and other social aspects of human
reproduction in order to prepare a "new breed" of health
personnel—gynecologic and nongynecologic—who will be able
to be more effective in these areas.

It is unlikely that adequate numbers of physicians can be
trained to perform the huge numbers of abortions, which
would be requested if there were no restrictive laws and until
family planning services become available to all those who
wish to use them. It is reasonable to assume, for example,
that the nurse-midwife, who, for more than fifteen years,
has been known to be trainable and competent in the management of normal pregnancy through and including delivery
and postpartum care, can also be trained to perform some
of the procedures for induced abortion, under the same medical supervision which guides her in her current responsibilities. It will also be necessary to document the possibility
of training obstetric-gynecologic nurses, or perhaps even
newer types of personnel, such as obstetric assistants trained
only in this area.

(4) Is preliminary psychiatric consultation necessary, if it
is not required by law? Is it, indeed, essential to good, medical
practice? Current practice originated historically in legal requirements. However, in the state of Maryland, where the
current law does not even mention the word "consultation,"
administrative medical practice continues to require psychiatric evaluation in patients with no previous psychiatric
illness, with no gross evidence of psychosis, but who simply
exhibit an intense desire to terminate a particular pregnancy.
Gynecologists have, for generations, been performing surgical
procedures which purposefully or inadvertently sterilize, fully
aware of an acknowledged but small incidence of adverse
psychological sequelae. Yet, psychiatric consultation has never

been required routinely, nor has it been considered part of appropriate medical practice.

It would seem necessary first to document whether or not the discernment of ambivalence toward pregnancy is an adequate prognosticator of adverse psychological sequelae. If studies would reveal that such is the case, it would then be necessary to document whether or not a board-certified or board-eligible psychiatrist is the only type of personnel who can make this evaluation. The alternatives could include non-psychiatric personnel, such as clinical psychologists, psychiatric nurses, psychiatric social workers, or mental health counselors. Finally, the question might be raised as to whether the gynecologist himself could do the evaluation just as effectively, with perhaps some additional training, in order to enable him to discern more precisely the patient who would genuinely benefit by psychiatric consultation. After all, judicious use of all highly trained specialists is an important consideration here as elsewhere.

(5) What is the impact of induced abortion on later, non-fatal complications? Long-term, follow-up studies are needed finally to determine whether these procedures are truly followed, in significant numbers of cases, by menstrual dysfunction, infertility, sterility, poor obstetrical outcome, and psychosexual or marital problems.

In conclusion, contemporary information regarding mortality, morbidity, and later, nonfatal sequelae to induced abortion, strongly suggest that these risks can be minimized, more by socio-medical improvements than by technological advances alone. Similar to the needs in improving general health care services in this country, the needs for improved services for induced abortion revolve around providing these services in safety, in comfort, and in dignity. General medical needs are devoid of one unique problem existing in the case of abortion—the need to convince our American culture of its propriety. This problem, however, will not be solved by research. It might be helped by some new directions in sexual education and orientation. What it will finally require is an awakening of our conscience and a greater acceptance of people as human beings with weaknesses and frailities common to us all.

# Discussion

**Hall:** The further we move along toward collecting statistics on abortion, the more I am concerned about the lack of uniformity in defining the various terms we are using. Not only are the definitions vague but they also differ from country to country, from state to state, and from community to community.

What is a septic abortion? What is a criminal abortion? It is even remarkably difficult to get uniform definitions of the duration of pregnancy. As abortion laws are changed, mortality and morbidity statistics associated with abortion will become more and more important; and yet, how do we define a death due to abortion?

Recently, Potts described deaths from abortion under the new British law. One woman who had a hospital abortion died about a month later from cancer of the rectum. There was uncertainty about whether to count this as a hospital abortion death. A Hungarian gynecologist said that he would attribute this death to abortion but his colleague, a statistician, who is involved in classifying deaths by cause, said that he would not report this as an abortion death.

New American state laws seem to require the reporting of different kinds of information to different agencies in each state. Abortion statistics by age for California, for example, cannot be compared with those for Georgia, because of differences in the age groups reported.

In view of these disparities and regardless of how statistics are maintained within a private or public organization, it is proposed that a central agency, ideally at the Federal level, be created to set uniform definitions and standards that would have to be met by those reporting data on abortions.

**Markush:** One of the problems in obtaining valid abortion statistics is that data on morbidity associated with abortion are almost nonexistent, and mortality data are very difficult to use. As long as classification systems are based on the underlying cause-of-death, or even on reported facts in the death certificate, it is exceedingly difficult to obtain accurate data on denominators. For example, no one seems to know why more deaths from heart disease are reported for nonwhite women than for other population groups. Heart disease appears to be a convenient catchall for all deaths. There is some soft evidence suggesting that heart disease is a diagnosis which shows ignorance rather than knowledge and, in effect, it means that the cause of death is often unknown. One of the possible explanations for the disproportionately high rate of heart disease reported for nonwhite women may be related, among other things, to illegal abortions. Nonwhite women who are poor and friendless and who have undergone illegal abortions are likely to be the ones who are not admitted to hospitals, and die at home. Until a few years ago, simple deliveries in some rural communities in the United States were performed by midwives. However, they were prohibited from handling complicated cases and such patients were to be admitted to hospitals. But the hospitals would not admit these women unless they could make an advance deposit. As a result, they were delivered at home without even the aid of midwives. In these circumstances, the morbidity or mortality data would seem to be quite undependable.

**Tietze:** In eastern and northern Europe, statistics on deaths from abortion in hospitals are based on a special system of reporting, unrelated to the general cause-of-death statistics, and, as a matter of principle, I believe this system is more suitable for arriving at the facts than trying to extract them from general cause-of-death statistics. Data on death from abortion, which are derived from cause-of-death statistics, have the reputation of being poor in general, even in Japan, where death statistics are excellent. Some well-informed people in Japan, like Muramatsu, feel that the true number of abortions may be three times higher than the reported number. Most of the abortions in Japan are performed in small outpatient clinics, run by individual physicians. It is claimed that the tax office checks on a physician's income and on the number of abortions he has reported and he may get into trouble if his tax declaration is out of line.

It would be possible to design a follow-back survey, using a sample which would give different weights to different types of data. I think I would probably take 100 percent of the deaths reported as due to causes associated with pregnancy and childbirth to ascertain whether something can be learned through a "psychological autopsy," and would sample the remaining death certificates for women of reproductive age. I would use a fairly small sample of deaths in hospitals because the temptation to prevaricate is pretty small by the time a woman gets into a hospital, and, particularly, if there were an autopsy. I would take about 30 to 50 percent of those who died out of hospital with a somewhat larger sample for younger unmarried and nonwhite women. However, such a study would be fiscally defensible only if it is set up as a major study of causes of death for women, rather than specifically for ascertaining the number of deaths from abortion.

**Sheps:** In this country it is difficult to do follow-up studies, because people move so often, a problem that may well be more acute in studying unmarried girls. It may not necessarily be so in the case of women who have fairly large families and whose reasons for wanting abortions are primarily economic. A follow-up of such cases depends in part on how much money and effort can be put into the study and whether inducements can be offered to the women to cooperate.

Another question that might be studied profitably concerns the characteristics of women who request abortions, the characteristics of their families, and the characteristics of those to whom abortion is granted or denied under various circumstances. What are the high-risk groups in relation to getting and not getting abortions in the first place?

In connection with risks associated with the duration of pregnancy, what characterizes a high-risk woman who has an abortion in the second trimester? It is obvious that the mortality risk is greater in the second trimester of pregnancy than in the first, but within that second trimester, we should be able to identify the characteristics that make the risk greater for some women than for others.

With regard to Rh sensitization and abortion, a study should be undertaken to ascertain whether there is a higher incidence of sensitization with one operative procedure than with another and whether the abortion helped to produce the sensitization.

**Seigel:** Rh sensitization is not independent of the operative procedure. Indeed, it is thought that sensitization occurs more frequently in the case of one type of procedure than another, as for example, with curettage versus suction. There is some suspicion that sensitization is a function of the operative procedure.

**Tietze:** Claims that one type of operation produces Rh sensitization more often than another type of operation have been made on the basis that more cases have been discovered over a number of years in those countries in which the suction method has come into use. Others have claimed that the classical D & C is involved because there is more bleeding due to more opening of blood vessels and, therefore, this would be more likely to produce Rh sensitization. However, the consensus is that it is a rare event and the main concern is with the woman who has not had her first baby before she is sensitized.

With regard to the availability of medical personnel and hospital beds for abortion, there are 80,000 obstetrical beds in this country and about 3.5 million deliveries a year. If each hospital bed were to be used by 50 women a year, 4 million deliveries could be accommodated. However, the average stay in hospitals for a delivery is much less than one week in the United States and, therefore, there must be vacant obstetrical hospital beds each year, which could be made available for abortions. There are, also, 20,000 obstetricians and gynecologists. If only one-half of them would do two abortions a week, which does not seem an impossible number, a million abortions would be provided for annually. Shortages of personnel and facilities, therefore, may not be a real issue, but, rather, an area of misapprehension.

**Cushner:** Although the medical, obstetrical, and gynecological societies in Maryland unanimously endorsed the bill before the legislature modified the abortion law, less than 10 percent of the membership are willing today to perform abortions. If the safety of outpatient procedures can be documented, arguments against utilization of hospital beds for abortion would be weakened because outpatient procedures not only reduce costs to the patient but do not require the use of hospital beds.

# SECTION II
# MENTAL HEALTH AND
# RELATED CONSIDERATIONS

# Therapeutic Abortion: A Liaison Psychiatrist's Perspective

Sanford R. Wolf, M.D.*

A NUMBER of states have recently revised their laws to permit therapeutic abortion on such psychiatric indications as the "preservation of the mental health" of the pregnant woman. Thus, psychiatrists are being drawn increasingly into the heated controversy of when and on whom abortion is to be performed.

Against the background of cultural change that is reshaping attitudes toward therapeutic abortion, this paper comments on the current dilemma facing psychiatrists and delineates future areas of investigation to expand our scant knowledge on this subject. The views herein reflect my three years' experience as the liaison psychiatrist to the Woman's Clinic of The Johns Hopkins Hospital. This paper also contains preliminary data and my clinical impressions based on 1,178 therapeutic abortions performed in that hospital during the year July 1968–June 1969.

* Formerly Department of Psychiatry and Center for Social Studies in Human Reproduction, The Johns Hopkins University School of Medicine, Baltimore, Maryland. Presently Assistant Professor and Director of Division of Liaison Psychiatry, Department of Psychiatry, School of Medicine, University of California San Diego, La Jolla, California.

## BACKGROUND

History is strewn with evidence that abortion has always been a subject of interest, if not of controversy. Provisions for abortion in almost all contemporary societies, and the rituals prescribed in these societies, lead one to suspect that attitudes toward abortion are a part of a universal cultural process in the same manner as attitudes toward puberty or mating.[1] Eastman has demonstrated the lack of historical correlation between the attitudes of societies toward abortion and their ethical conduct or intellectual sophistication.[2]

Our own attitudes toward abortion are thought to be derived from the commandment "Thou shalt not kill," and its Judeo-Christian interpretation. Jacobovitz has traced the difference between Jewish and Catholic attitudes toward abortion to the erroneous translation of a single sentence in the book of Exodus by the early Christians.[3] This mistranslation was incorporated into early Christian dogma by the third century theologian, Tertullian, because of his ignorance of Hebrew; and, from there, was passed into early canon law.

The many complex religious arguments and decrees, which attempted to define at which stage of gestation a fetus becomes a person, are far beyond the scope of this paper. Suffice it to say that the argument continued for many centuries and that the present position of the Catholic Church was adopted as recently as 1869.

A major factor in the evolution of present-day attitudes toward abortion has its origin in the gradual breakdown of the repressive sexual mores of the Victorian Age. An important cause of this change, and one which has received little attention, is the devastating effect of the First World War, which left in its wake disillusionment and loss of hope in a social system whose values, buttressed by a Victorian moral code, had brought on the slaughter.[4]

In the decade that followed the First World War, sexual

mores became more permissive, and matters pertaining to sexuality were more openly discussed. This was the time that saw the spread of the previously persecuted Planned Parenthood movement, led by Margaret Sanger. In this decade of "de-repression of feelings," the ideas of Freud, one of the first to speak out in a forceful manner in favor of contraception and responsible parenthood, spread rapidly among psychiatrists and the lay public.[5]

In the decades that followed World War I, the subject of abortion was relegated to the background, while controversy over birth control was waged in the open. Public discussion of abortion emerged only as resistance to birth control began to recede.

## INVOLVEMENT OF THE PSYCHIATRIST

The majority of abortions performed on psychiatric recommendation do not appear to be "strictly psychiatric," if this term is defined as the presence of deeply ingrained neurotic or psychotic traits or the certain danger of suicide. The symptoms presented by patients in such circumstances usually consist of a variety of personality disorders, impulsive behavior, misjudgment, or excessive use of such defenses as denial, which interact with environmental concerns, resulting in severe, but often transient, emotional upheaval. Similar blends of intrapsychic and social issues also characterize many other areas of psychiatric interest, such as forensic psychiatry, alchoholism, drug addiction, and some types of adolescent behavior. Patients in these situations who experience marked psychic turmoil, whether or not they are diagnosed as having discrete, circumscribed psychiatric illness, are proper subjects for observation and therapeutic treatment.

This paper does not purport to define specific psychodynamic factors that should be explored or weighed in determining whether or not a psychiatrist recommend that an abortion be performed on an individual patient. Such a recommendation can only be considered in the context of the unique life experiences of each woman and her family.[6]

When a psychiatrist is face to face with the issue of therapeutic abortion in a specific case, the most important consideration in his mind is the total effect on the woman and her family of carrying the pregnancy to term versus the effect of the abortion itself. Because psychosocial sequelae, which may follow either course the woman and her psychiatrist choose, have never been systematically explored, no basis exists for understanding these sequelae, which are frequently expressed in terms of vague rumor, anecdote, and uncertainty.

## RESEARCH CONSIDERATIONS

Many psychiatrists have urged that carefully controlled clinical studies be undertaken to determine the nature of psychosocial sequelae under various circumstances. However, no one has yet dealt in depth with those factors to be considered in order to conduct a "carefully controlled clinical study." The following are some methodological and theoretical issues which must be taken into consideration before a study can be designed that is likely to provide useful data for the future.

### 1. SELECTION OF STUDY GROUPS

To understand the sequelae of pregnancy or abortion, it is necessary to study large numbers of women and their families, and then to group them by selected characteristics. Although each person's response to pregnancy is unique, this grouping is the only realistic method which would allow us to evolve general guidelines for use by psychiatrists when they are clinically confronted with the possibility of abortion in a particular patient whose personality and life circumstances tend to approximate those of a previously defined group.

Vast differences may be found in the emotional impact

that pregnancy or its termination has on a woman depending on her personality, age, parity, and environmental circumstances. For example, there is no reason to expect that, other things being equal, a woman with a consciously unwanted pregnancy who is aborted in humiliating and illicit circumstances will react in the same manner as a woman with a similar problem aborted in the supportive conditions of a hospital. Within the group of women aborted in hospitals, there is even less reason to conclude that a woman who may very much want to continue her pregnancy, but must be aborted because of severe renal disease, will react in the same manner as a woman who rejects pregnancy and chooses abortion for emotional reasons. Thus, any study of abortion which has as its principal aim the understanding of sequelae must compare reasonably similar groups of women. Largely because of the limited number of cases in the United States, it has not been possible to conduct a valid study. Conclusions drawn from earlier reports, therefore, are unreliable and sometimes ambiguous. Psychological reactions to abortion reported in the literature up to 1966 have been reviewed and criticized by Simon and Senturia.[7] This literature is most noteworthy for the paucity of data on sequelae and for the inconsistency with which such information is reported.

Such a study would best be accomplished by comparing groups of women matched for: age, parity, race, socioeconomic status, marital status, legality of abortion, stage of gestation, whether the abortion was for psychosocial or medical reasons, the type of operative procedure used, and the psychological status and psychiatric diagnosis of the patient. Each of these matching criteria may be a unique indicator of a woman's reaction to abortion.

*Age and Parity*

Many authors reporting on the sequelae of abortion do not mention the age and parity of the patients. When age is mentioned, conclusions are often drawn from women of vastly different ages.[8] Moreover, a number of narrative accounts of the sequelae of abortion which have taken note of age and parity tend to be conflicting.[9]

The preliminary data derived from therapeutic abortions performed at The Johns Hopkins Hospital suggest that women in their thirties who had already borne children and who sought abortion for some compelling emotional reason generally handled the entire procedure and the period of convalescence more easily than younger women who had borne no children.

*Socioeconomic Circumstances*

Although clinical reports concerning abortion in the United States have paid little heed to the vast cultural and economic differences between various women seeking this procedure, evidence exists of a definite class and racial bias in the granting of hospital abortions. Reports indicate that proportionately fewer therapeutic abortions are performed on clinic patients compared with private patients, and, similarly, fewer on Negro compared with white patients.[10] Other factors, however, may account for this difference. For example, Rainwater's excellent descriptive study of pregnancy and its value in the self-image of the urban, Negro poor can be interpreted to show that circumstances other than finances and level of education account for the lower incidence of therapeutic abortion among Negro patients.[11]

*Type of Operative Procedure*

No report on the psychosocial sequelae of abortion has given cognizance to the manner in which the procedure was carried out. During dilatation and curettage, as well as suction aspiration, which can rarely be employed later than the twelfth week of pregnancy, the patient is under anesthesia during the brief procedure. A newer procedure which allows therapeutic abortion to be carried out from the sixteenth week on through intra-amniotic instillation of hypertonic saline solution may be prolonged for many hours; pain somewhat like that felt in childbirth may be experienced; and the patient is awake for all but the final stages.[12]

### Criminal or Legal Abortion

The element of illegality adds a measure of guilt to what already is a difficult experience. Ironically, this point was underscored at a national conference on abortion by a physician who, himself, had spent most of his professional career performing abortions in a manner that was judged outside the law.[13]

### Abortions Performed for Medical or Psychosocial Reasons

In nearly all cases where abortion is performed for psychosocial reasons, the woman has initiated the request, and, at least on a conscious level, the pregnancy has been rejected. In abortions performed for organic medical reasons, the situation can be quite different.

### Psychologic Status and Diagnosis

While understanding that the psychologic dynamics operating in each patient and her family are unique, study purposes necessitate that common areas of conflict, defense, or diagnosis be defined to allow for the grouping of patients according to the principal emotional aspects involved in each case and to the intensity of these symptoms. A careful, standardized psychologic evaluation should be carried out before abortion. In longitudinal follow-up studies, it should be possible to determine which of the types of conflict or diagnostic groups result in more or less serious sequelae. Such longitudinal studies must be carefully and systematically carried out, since sequelae discerned at follow-up may simply be a reiteration of psychodynamic factors that antecede the abortion. There is some evidence that the basic emotional difficulties found on follow-up after abortion are directly related to the patient's preabortion mental state.[14]

It is evident that if all the factors mentioned above are taken into consideration in determining the sequelae to abortion in groups matched for selected characteristics, the reactions of many individual women will have to be studied. The numbers of cases needed may be beyond the resources of any medical group or hospital. A state registry, such as the one adopted in Colorado, should be useful in carrying out such a study.[15]

## 2. DIFFICULTY IN UTILIZING CONTROL GROUPS

A control group to be compared to a group of women undergoing abortion is not possible in the strict experimental sense; i.e., all variables but one (abortion) being held constant. The psychodynamic and environmental factors which lead one woman to request abortion and another, for example, to have her child adopted, may in themselves define these women as different prior to any study of sequelae. Nevertheless, much valuable data might be obtained by comparing the sequelae among women dealing with the life crisis of unwanted pregnancy through different means. The data thus obtained could be of assistance to therapists in the development of predictive tools for gauging future behavior in their patients.

## 3. DISTORTIONS INHERENT IN CONCLUDING SEQUELAE IN THE GENERAL POPULATION ON THE BASIS OF OLDER CLINICAL PSYCHIATRIC REPORTS

For the purposes of designing a study on the sequelae of abortion, little reliance can be placed on the older clinical psychiatric reports frequently quoted. These reports deal with data obtained from patients who have chosen to enter psychotherapy and who, during the course of therapy, have brought up various matters relating to an earlier abortion.[16] The reports have provided much useful psychodynamic knowledge on the psychology of women. However, in extending their findings to the general population, the problem of self-selection arises. Patients who present themselves or are referred to a psychiatrist do so because of some emotional problem, while those women who had been aborted and suffered no sequelae are not heard from.

A second problem in relying heavily on these older clinical reports is historic in nature. Until recently, it was quite common to perform sterilization concurrently with abortion.[17] We know from clinical experience that sterilization, especially if forced on an unwilling woman, is likely to result in emotional sequelae of its own.[18]

4. INTERVIEW SITUATION

Because therapeutic abortion is the only medical procedure subject to criminal codes, a distortion is built into the doctor-patient transaction. This is especially true in those states where therapeutic abortion is allowed to preserve the life of the woman only. In these states, the woman who for any reason feels she must be aborted is under extreme pressure to prove she is suicidal. In those states where abortion is permissible in order to protect the physical or mental health of the woman, this built-in distorting factor is greatly lessened, but still present.

In any event, even with more "liberal" laws, when a psychiatrist evaluates a woman who is determined to be aborted, her need for a secondary gain places a pressure upon his thoughts and judgment, though even in these distorted situations an evaluation can be performed by a competent clinician. Nevertheless, the evaluation and the administrative procedures leading to abortion are often so prolonged and strained that they, in themselves, might be a proper subject for psychosocial research.

## DISCUSSION

As states revise their laws governing the performance of therapeutic abortion to include, as legal grounds for abortion, "psychiatric" or "mental health" factors and social and environmental factors, the stigma attached to illegitimacy will be taken strongly into consideration, whether or not this factor is specifically indicated by law. Prior to 1965, the majority of therapeutic abortions in American hospitals were performed on married women.[19] This situation has now been reversed in many hospitals under revised laws. For example, data on the initial 496 therapeutic abortions performed at The Johns Hopkins Hospital, since July, 1968, under the revised Maryland code, reveal that 73 percent of the women were single, divorced, separated, or widowed. In reviewing the experience at Denver General Hospital in the first eleven months after passage of the revised Colorado abortion code, 86 percent of the 109 cases involved unmarried women.[20]

It is interesting to compare the present American experience with that of Scandinavia where "social" indications have long been considered for therapeutic abortion. However, these "social" indications appear to be quite different from those operating in the United States. The most striking example is that the proportion of unmarried women who are aborted in the United States under the revised laws is considerably larger than the proportion of unmarried women aborted under Scandinavia's more liberal codes. In Scandinavia, approximately 70 percent of the therapeutic abortions are performed on married women.[21] The "exhausted housewife" syndrome or the "stress syndrome of housewives" is considered a much more important factor in the permitting of abortion than are the problems arising from pregnancy in an unmarried woman, especially a young woman. Therapeutic abortion in this last group is discouraged.

For this reason, it would seem difficult to compare the extensive work done on abortion sequelae in the Scandinavian countries[22] with the contemporary American situation in states with liberalized laws, since different factors appear to be operating.

It is probable that, in the future, changes will occur which will remove the laws governing therapeutic abortion from the legal codes and place the decision on abortion within the doctor-patient relationship. It has been stated by some that the present restrictive laws are unconstitutional and that they violate the Fourth Amendment.[23]

It is ironic that those opposed to this change justify their views by saying that not enough information is available on the sequelae of induced abortion, and careful studies are needed. This is, I believe, circular reasoning. Laws governing abortion have themselves been a principal deterrent to the execution of careful clinical research on psychosocial sequelae. Moreover, as the various sequelae to abortion are explored, it is being repeatedly noted that they are far less traumatic than once believed. Such information is, in itself, bound to accelerate doubts as to the relevance of restrictive abortion laws.

The role of the psychiatrist in cases of abortion should evolve as experience and knowledge are accumulated. Given the reality of present-day abortion laws, including those considered liberal, psychiatrists should concentrate on documentation and follow-up of the various ways in which different women deal with unwanted pregnancy. It is upon this knowledge that the psychiatrist will lean most heavily whenever individual patients are seen in evaluation or treatment. In the future, hopefully, the psychiatrist will gradually assume what should be his only role in respect to abortion. In such a role, consultation would be available and advisable, though not mandatory, enabling the psychiatrist to work with the patient in clarifying her conscious and unconscious motives and defenses. The patient would then be able to make her own appropriate decision on the termination of pregnancy with the widest self-knowledge and awareness of those psychic determinants which have entered into her choice.

## NOTES

1. Devereux, G., *A Study of Abortion in Primitive Societies* (New York: Julian Press, 1955), pp. x, 1–394.

2. Eastman, N. J., "Induced abortion and contraception," *Obstetrical Gynecological Survey,* 22:3–11 (February 1967).

3. Jacobovitz, I., "The Jewish views on abortion," *Abortion and the Law* (ed. D. T. Smith) (Cleveland, Ohio: Western Reserve University Press, 1967), pp. 124–143.

4. Tuchman, B. W., *The Guns of August* (New York: Dell Publishing Co., 1963), pp. 347–362 (paperback).

5. Freud, S., "Sexuality in the aetiology of the neurosis (1898)," *The Standard Edition of the Complete Works of Sigmund Freud, Volume 3* (London: Hogarth Press, 1953), pp. 263–285.

6. Aarons, Z. A., "Therapeutic abortion and the psychiatrist," *American Journal of Psychiatry,* 124:745–754 (December 1967).

7. Simon, N. M., and Senturia, A., "Psychiatric sequelae of abortion: review of the literature, 1935–1964," *Archives of General Psychiatry,* 15: 378–389 (October 1966).

8. Hamilton, V. C., "Some sociologic and psychologic observations on abortion: a study of 537 cases," *American Journal of Obstetrics and Gynecology,* 39:919–928 (June 1940); "Medical status and psychologic attitudes of patients following abortion: a follow-up of 100 cases," *American Journal of Obstetrics and Gynecology,* 41:285–288 (February 1941).

9. Dunbar, F., "A psychosomatic approach to abortion and the abortion habit," *Therapeutic Abortion* (ed. H. Rosen) (New York: Julian Press, 1954), pp. 22–31; Deutsch, H., *Psychology of Women, Vol. II, Motherhood* (New York: Grune and Stratton, 1945), pp. 179–201.

10. Hall, R. E., "Therapeutic abortion, sterilization, and contraception," *American Journal of Obstetrics and Gynecology,* 91:518–532 (February 15, 1965); Tietze, C., "Therapeutic abortion in the United States, *American Journal of Obstetrics and Gynecology,* 101:784–787 (July 15, 1968).

11. Rainwater, L., "The Negro family: the crucible of identity," *Daedalus,* 95:172–216 (Winter 1966).

12. Jaffin, H., Kerenyi, T., and Wood, E. C., "Termination of missed abortion and the induction of labor in midtrimester pregnancy," *American Journal of Obstetrics and Gynecology,* 84:602–608 (September 1, 1962); Johnson, J. W. C.; Cushner, I. M.; and Stephens, N. L.: "Hazards of using hypertonic saline for therapeutic abortion," *American Journal of Obstetrics and Gynecology,* 94:225–229 (January 15, 1966); Fuchs, F., "Termination of pregnancy by intraamniotic injection of hypertonic solutions," *Advances in Obstetrics and Gynecology, Volume 1* (ed. S. L. Marcus and C. C. Marcus) (Baltimore: Williams and Wilkins, 1967), pp. 258–270.

13. Timanus, G. L., "Final discussion," *Abortion in the United States*

(ed. M. S. Calderone) (New York: Hoeber-Harper, 1958), pp. 169–172.

14. Jansson, B., "Mental disorders after abortion," *Acta psychiatrica Scandinavica*, 41:87–110 (1965).

15. Heller, A., and Whittington, H. G., "The Colorado story: Denver General Hospital experience with the change in the law on therapeutic abortion," *American Journal of Psychiatry*, 125:806–816 (December 1968).

16. Dunbar, "Psychosomatic approach to abortion," pp. 22–31; Deutsch, *Psychology of Women*, pp. 179–201; Hall, "Therapeutic abortion," pp. 518–532; Romm, M. E., "Psychoanalytic considerations," *Therapeutic Abortion* (ed. H. Rosen) (New York: Julian Press, 1954), pp. 209–212.

17. Taussig, F. J., *Abortion, Spontaneous and Induced, Medical and Social Aspects* (St. Louis, Mo.: Mosby, 1936), pp. 341–351, 446–452; Rosen, H., "The emotionally sick patient: psychiatric indications and contraindications to the interruption of pregnancy," *Therapeutic Abortion* (ed. H. Rosen) (New York: Julian Press, 1954), pp. 219–243; Wilson, D. C., "The abortion problem in the general hospital," *Therapeutic Abortion* (ed. H. Rosen) (New York: Julian Press, 1954), pp. 189–197.

18. Rosen, "The emotionally sick patient," pp. 219–243; Barnes, A. E., and Zuspan, F. P., "Patient reaction to puerperal surgical sterilization," *American Journal of Obstetrics and Gynecology*, 75:65–71 (January 1958); Barglow, P., "Pseudocyesis and psychiatric sequelae of sterilization," *Archives of General Psychiatry*, 11:571–580 (December 1964).

19. Taussig, *Abortion, Spontaneous and Induced*, pp. 341–351, 446–452; Niswander, K. R.; Klein, M.; and Randall, C. L., "Changing attitudes toward therapeutic abortions," *Journal of the American Medical Association*, 196:1140–1143 (June 27, 1966).

20. Heller and Whittington, "The Colorado Study," pp. 806–816.

21. Skalts, V., and Norgaard, M., "Abortion legislation in Denmark," *Abortion and the Law* (ed. D. T. Smith) (Cleveland, Ohio: Western Reserve University Press, 1967), pp. 144–178; Höök, K., "Refused abortion: a follow-up study of 249 women whose applications were refused by the National Board of Health in Sweden," *Acta psychiatrica Scandinavica*, 39 (suppl. 168):1–156 (1963).

22. Höök, "Refused abortion," pp. 1–156; Arén, P., and Åmark, C., "The prognosis in cases in which legal abortion has been granted but not carried out," *Acta psychiatrica et neurologica Scandinavica*, 36:203–278 (1961); Ekblad, M., "Induced abortion on psychiatric grounds: a follow-up study of 479 women," *Acta psychiatrica et neurologica Scandinavica*, suppl. 99:1–238 (1955).

23. Rossi, Alice S., *Social Change and Abortion Law Reform*. Paper presented at the American Orthopsychiatric Association, March 21, 1968.

# The Child Born after Denial of Abortion Request

Edward Pohlman, Ph.D.*

THE CHILD born after his mother's request for abortion had been denied (hereafter to be designated CADAR) is part of that broader category known as the unwanted child. No airtight scientific evidence exists that unwanted conceptions, per se, have less desirable effects for mother or child than wanted conceptions.[1] However, if it is true, as British data suggest, that abortion was much more frequent among women with unwanted conceptions than among other pregnant women, and if induced abortions have some undesirable consequences for some parents, then, this is the clearest piece of evidence we have that unwanted conceptions have adverse effects.[2]

In a Swedish study, more behavior problems were claimed among CADARs than among the controls.[3] But since 27 percent of the CADARs were born out of wedlock, compared with 7.5 percent for the controls, it is not justifiable to use the study as proof of adverse effects in cases in which abortions are refused. It might be worthwhile to re-analyze these data, making separate comparisons among the in-wedlock CADAR-control pairs only, or among the 86 pairs (out of 120) where the marital status was the same among CADAR and control children.

* Professor of Educational and Counseling Psychology, University of the Pacific, Stockton, California.

Every child, whether wanted or unwanted, adds to population and to population problems. It is also true that unsuccessful attempts to induce abortion may produce direct physical damage to the mother and fetus, varying from minor to severe and permanent. Unsuccessful abortion attempts may also upset the mother emotionally and may interfere with the mother-child relationship. In a sense, and from the standpoint of public health, harmful effects of clumsy unsuccessful efforts at abortion should also be attributed to refusals of requests for legal, expert abortion.

Since, thus far, research in this area has been minimal, there is little evidence that unwanted conceptions are "bad" for either parents or children. Nevertheless, a number of logical channels exist which suggest that unwanted conceptions or abortion-refusals might theoretically lead to adverse effects. For example, it seems probable that such emotions as severe rage may hurt the fetus perceptibly.[4] A set of hypotheses may, with slight modifications, be applied to the possible undesirable effects of: (1) children of the "wrong" sex; (2) children born at the wrong time; that is, too early or too late; (3) children conceived out of wedlock; (4) children born out of wedlock; (5) larger versus smaller families; (6) CADARs; (7) children unwanted before conception; and (8) certain other groups—in each case with appropriate controls.[5]

## DEFINITIONS

"Wanted" and "unwanted" suggest a dichotomy; but a continuum between extreme rejection and extreme acceptance is more appropriate. Still, a single continuum is not completely satisfactory. When conscious and unconscious feelings differ—usually repressed hatred masked by overt acceptance—the unconscious factors should probably be used in classifying cases. But how can we place, on one dimension, the feelings of two parents who disagree, the child who perceives his parents' feelings wrongly, or the child who is truly wanted but for "sick" reasons? We might average the feelings of two disagreeing parents and weight the score by their importance in the child's life, and possibly add weights for other influential family members, to arrive at a "Rejection Quotient." Throughout this paper, however, the term "unwanted" will be used to refer to one extreme on a hypothetical continuum.

Because parents' feelings change over time, we suggest the following categories referring to four units of unwantedness in terms of time: (1) unwanted before conception occurred, (2) unwanted during the first trimester of pregnancy when abortion is easier to obtain than later in pregnancy, (3) unwanted during the second and third trimesters, and (4) unwanted immediately after birth (Table 1).

These categories are designated "unwanted conception," "unwanted abortion potential," "unwanted pregnancy," and "unwanted infant," referring to the earliest point concerning which a measure of the unwanted-wanted status can be obtained, either in a prospective study or retrospectively. The use of a Rejection Quotient, together with any one of the four categories, would make these measurements extremely complex.

The child unwanted before conception but supposedly wanted later may, in a sense, still be an unwanted child within the meaning of the first category. In general, he is more likely to be unconsciously unwanted, during pregnancy or at any later point, than the child who was wanted before conception. Very soon after the pregnancy is discovered, the process of rationalization may begin. The principal explanation for the extensive shifts from rejection of the pregnancy to its acceptance seems to be rationalization, although some individuals may have "genuine" shifts in feelings in either direction. Further research on the consistency of parental feelings over time would be of great importance to those interested in primary prevention.[6]

## TABLE 1.
## FOUR TYPES OF UNWANTED UNITS

| Earliest time of unwanted feelings | Informal term | Formal term, subscript* | If a child is born | Parallel term for parent(s) |
|---|---|---|---|---|
| Before conception | Unwanted conception | Unwanted unit$_c$ | Unwanted child$_c$ | Unwanting parent$_c$ |
| First trimester after conception | Unwanted abortion potential | Unwanted unit$_a$ | Unwanted child$_a$ | Unwanting parent$_a$ |
| Later pregnancy after first trimester | Unwanted pregnancy | Unwanted unit$_p$ | Unwanted child$_p$ | Unwanting parent$_p$ |
| After birth at some time | Unwanted infant | Unwanted unit$_i$ | Unwanted child$_i$ | Unwanting parent$_i$ |

Note: Classified according to the earliest time concerning which unwanting feelings on the parent's part are established by research (either through retrospective questions such as "Did you at that time want . . ." or through prospective, longitudinal questions such as, "Do you now want . . ." (The terms "unwanted" & "unwanting" incorrectly imply a simple dichotomy.)

* Subscripts $c$, $a$, $p$, $i$ refer to parallel line under heading Informal term.

## KINDS OF STUDIES POSSIBLE

Six types of studies of unwanted children are suggested in Table 2. Though not a comprehensive list, it serves to illustrate some of the major possibilities. The listing is divided into retrospective and prospective studies, and then further subdivided, in Columns **X, Y,** and **Z,** into studies of whether abortion was formally requested and denied, studies where parents are asked whether they desire or would have desired an abortion, and studies where parents are asked whether they really want or wanted another conception. The specific questions listed in the columns are intended to be illustrative and thematic, and might serve as a basis for a carefully designed scale.

Obviously, the hypotheses of greatest interest would involve contrasting the unwanted child with appropriate controls. But a number of other hypotheses may be suggested. (1) A decrease in the average "Rejection Quotient" would occur from Column **X** to Column **Y,** and from **Y** to **Z,** with a corresponding increase in the standard deviation. In other words, under present legal circumstances with regard to abortion in the United States, those actually seeking abortion are more rejecting of the pregnancy, and more homogeneous in their rejection, than those merely wishing an abortion, and both are more rejecting of the pregnancy and more homogeneous in their rejection than those merely claiming that conception was unwanted. (2) Those requesting abortion for physical reasons (e.g., rubella, thalidomide, or the woman's physical health) may be less rejecting of the pregnancy than are those requesting abortion for other reasons, and, if this proves correct, should be excluded in most comparisons. (3) Among individuals with similar Rejection Quotients, those who believe abortion morally wrong would be less likely to request abortion. If this hypothesis is valid, studies of Column **X**

## TABLE 2.
### SIX TYPES OF RESEARCH ON UNWANTED CHILDREN

| | X Abortion request denied | Y Abortion desired | Z Conception unwanted before it occurred |
|---|---|---|---|
| 1 Retrospective | X-1 Either self-report ("Did you request an abortion & have request denied?") or objective study of available records | Y-1 Self-report ("At that time, if you could have had an abortion with no risks to health & life of mother, would you . . . ?") | Z-1 Self-report ("At that time, would you rather not have had another (or "a") conception just then, if you could have had what you wanted?") |
| 2 Prospective-longitudinal | X-2 Starts during pregnancy. Either self-report or available independent records, as above | Y-2 Starts during pregnancy. Self-report, as above ("If you could now have . . .") | Z-2 Starts before conception with large sample to allow for those who never get pregnant. Self-report ("Would you like to have another . . .") |

parents and controls could remove a source of variance by restricting samples to those who believed abortion morally acceptable. (4) The higher the motivation, the more psychological and environmental barriers the couple or woman will surmount to get the abortion. (5) The more relaxed the abortion legislation, and the more tolerant the society's mores with regard to abortion, the lower will be the average Rejection Quotient of those who have abortions.

## DANGERS IN GENERALIZING FROM SAMPLES

If, as hypothesized above, groups in Columns X, Y, and Z represent different kinds of people and differ in their Rejection Quotients, then findings for one group cannot be generalized safely to another. Parents in Column X, who presumably want abortions very much, are probably more rejecting of pregnancy than the average parent who would get an abortion if laws were relaxed greatly. On the other hand, parents in Column Y may actually be more representative of the parents who would be in Column X, if laws were relaxed. A demonstration of serious harm resulting from refusals for abortions for families now in Column X would not prove that similar serious effects are now accruing to families in Column Y simply because abortions are not more available to the latter group. Perhaps the relatively small percentage of very miserable people who now apply for abortions in the states with restrictive abortion legislation are not only exceedingly difficult to study but also may not be representative of the average couple who would get an abortion if abortions were more easily available. More relevant, perhaps, are samples from states with newly liberalized or recently repealed abortion legislation.

Generalization of findings is further restricted because of many subgroups among those requesting or desiring abortion, such as the single versus the married, wives with marital versus extramarital conceptions, women of different parities, women of different ages, the seriously psychiatrically disturbed versus the normal, and those requesting abortions for more strictly physical reasons versus more economic-social-psychological reasons.

## CRITERIA FOR DECIDING PRIORITIES AMONG RESEARCH

We suggest four criteria for guidance in determining research priorities in studies of unwanted children: (1) practical relevance to (a) family planning, (b) population control, and (c) health status, (2) public information and public relations value, (3) value in predicting outcomes of approved versus refused abortions, and (4) feasibility in research design, execution, and cost.

### PRACTICAL RELEVANCE
In the tabulation of categories of unwantedness according to time, shown above, the first two categories appear to have more practical relevance than the last two categories, studies of which would not appreciably affect decisions about action, regardless of the findings. They also seem to have less value for public relations and information. For these reasons, only the first two of the four categories on unwantedness related to time—that is, unwanted before conception, or during the first trimester of pregnancy—were used in the six types of studies of unwanted children proposed above and will be discussed here.

### PUBLIC RELATIONS AND INFORMATION
The struggle for public acceptance of contraception has progressed much further than the fight for public acceptance of abortion. Many people already believe that unwanted conceptions are "bad" and should be prevented by contraception. Far fewer believe that forced childbirth by abortion-refusal is "bad." Hence, the public information criterion

would seem to give priority to Columns **X** and **Y** studies over Column **Z** studies.

### PREDICTING OUTCOMES

If there is a large increase in the number of abortions in the United States, the question of psychiatric consultation, of the predictive validity of interviews by psychiatrists and others, and of tests will increase in importance. Hence, there will be a great need for studies that help predict what happens when abortion is performed or denied. Aside from decisions about individuals, we need to know on an epidemiological and public health level the effects, especially psychological effects, of abortion and abortion denial on the women and men involved, on existing children if any, and, in the case of abortion refusal, on the child.

### FEASIBILITY

Columns **Z** type studies, involving unwanted conceptions, seem less feasible than Column **Y** type studies, for reasons which will be reviewed in the section on "difficulties with research on unwanted conception" below. In any case, much of the information available from Column **Z** type studies can be obtained from Column **Y** type studies, and by selected use of data from European studies of the Column **X** type. Study subjects who belong in Column **Y** probably belong in Column **Z** as well, although the reverse may not be true.

## DIFFICULTIES WITH RESEARCH ON UNWANTED CONCEPTIONS

Column **Z** type studies present grave difficulties. If a retrospective format is used, as in **Z-1**, four problems are met with: (1) Parents are not always sure how to answer questions because they honestly do not know how to *define* "unwanted" conceptions. If experts are confused about this concept, surely parents must be even more confused. (2) Parents *forget* whether they wanted the child before its conception, or whether they were practicing contraception at the time of conception. (3) Parents distort their memories in line with their emotional needs, *repressing* the memory that the conception was unwanted. (4) Parents deliberately *prevaricate* to interviewers, claiming a conception was wanted when they remember that it was not wanted. These four problems would probably invalidate a control group much more than the study group. Evidence from the longitudinal study of Westoff, *et al.* suggests that parents are more likely to "change" their memories and/or their statements toward acceptance of a previously rejected pregnancy than *vice versa*.[7] The longitudinal sweep of this study was between two points in time after the birth of a child, and thus did not cover the period when changes in feelings about pregnancy are presumably much greater.

One approach to avoiding these problems is through Z-2 studies, that is, longitudinal studies of unwanted conceptions. This type of study, however, is complicated because one must start with a large group of women who are not now pregnant and ask whether they want another child, and then wait until a certain proportion who do not want a child get pregnant anyway. Sample shrinkage would be considerable. Furthermore, skill, patience, time, and money are required while waiting for unwanted conceptions to occur. Such considerations have prompted me to suggest previously that we virtually eliminate Column Z type studies as a research focus, although this opinion may be prematurely pessimistic.[8]

It is not unreasonable to estimate that one-fifth of the babies born in wedlock are unwanted by some moderate definition, and the total number of unwanted babies, including those born out-of-wedlock, runs close to a million a year. If unwanted conceptions produce undesirable consequences, these consequences are present on an enormous scale, and the public health problems implied might be staggering, though hidden. Perhaps it is vital to prove the assumed relationships and publicize them; perhaps we need to keep hammering away at some means of doing Column **Z** type studies as such. But the difficulties and dollar costs are tremendous, and Column **Z** type studies seem to deserve lower priority than those in Columns **X** and **Y**.

For adequate execution of Column **Z** type studies, at least one major longitudinal study would seem necessary. Among women who become pregnant after the initial interview, periodic reinterviews early in the pregnancy, and again later in pregnancy and after birth, would provide a picture of stability or change in feelings. Later studies could utilize these findings because we would then know the accuracy, within fairly precise limits, of the mother's retrospective claims that she did or did not want the baby at some earlier time, including before conception. In other words, such a longitudinal study could answer the now unanswered question of whether we can rely on the mothers' retrospective statements and safely start other longitudinal studies without going back to the period before conception. The proposed longitudinal study would follow up on a mass of dependent variables over the years, as implied throughout this paper.

A less expensive and less satisfactory longitudinal study would start with currently pregnant women and then move along the lines already indicated. The question of whether conception was wanted could be routinely asked on confidential hospital admission forms and on other types of medical, social, and psychological records. This is especially applicable to forms filled out early in pregnancy and forms dealing with the "battered child." Some forms could also include questions as to whether abortion was requested or denied at previous pregnancies.

## DIFFICULTIES WITH RECORDS OF
## ABORTION DENIAL

Many of the problems noted above for Column **Z** type studies are bypassed if we rely on the question of whether or not abortion was formally requested, as stated in Column **X**. We may bypass parents' memories and self-reporting completely, if we have access to formal records, as did Forssman and Thuwe.[9] Or, if we must rely on the parents' reports, the question of whether or not they formally applied for an abortion is a relatively easy peg on which to hang their reports or their memories, leaving less ambiguity as to definition than Column **Z** type questions. Perhaps high priority should be given to studies in Scandinavia and eastern Europe, which compare CADARs and controls, both in retrospective and prospective designs. One such study is currently in progress.[10]

In the United States, studies of abortion denial, as such, pose other problems. Those denied abortion are often more furtive and elusive than their European counterparts, and centralized records of their experiences and whereabouts are nonexistent. Irritation over abortion denial may make women especially reluctant to cooperate. With removal or liberalization of antiabortion legislation, the picture may improve, but at present direct research in the United States on the woman to whom an abortion has been denied, or on her family (CADARs), is very difficult indeed.

## DIFFICULTIES WITH REPORTS THAT ABORTION IS DESIRED

Studies asking parents whether they would have liked an abortion are probably much more feasible in the United States than studies of abortion requests which have been denied. And the question "Would you have liked an abortion" has some advantage over the question "Did you want this conception" because it provides a clearer operational definition to work with. A prospective study (**Y-2**) would provide for interviews with a large number of women early in pregnancy and ask whether an abortion would be wanted now, if available. Such a question would need to be preceded by an explanation, such as, "we are extremely sorry that we cannot make abortion available to those who want it, but doctors would be interested in knowing how you would feel if abortion were available to you in a completely legal way and with medical safety." This type of question would bring into sharper focus the definition of unwantedness than if mothers were merely asked if they wanted the pregnancy.

A major advantage of Y-2 over Z-2 type studies is that they can start during pregnancy, instead of starting before conception and waiting for unwanted pregnancies to occur. If the key focus of a particular study is on effects of abortion denial, Y-2 studies are more directly relevant than Z-2 studies. And for public relations and public information purposes, Y-2 studies seem much more relevant than do Z-2 studies.

## *ALTERNATIVES TO RESEARCH*

Influencing public opinion is important. But not all efforts toward this end need be spent on new and rigidly controlled research. The proverbial mole died trying to dig his way to the point the eagle could see all along. Existing data, where available, can be collected and studied and through serendipity may reveal patterns that would be hard to contradict. These can be made available to the public even before the scientific research needed to prove them is completed. It may take years to complete the research, and educated tentative conclusions are needed immediately for purposes of public information. It is better that policy be decided on the basis of tentative conclusions reached by experts on incomplete evidence than that it be decided by the less-informed, without any evidence and possibly on the basis of myths, prejudices, and guesses. The scientist who keeps himself pure by walking away from any question where evidence is incomplete, leaving decisions to the bystander, is irresponsible. For example, the assertion that maternal deaths from abortion would be reduced by removing the legal condemnation against abortion is a powerful argument and should be made loudly. Similarly, the assertion that unsuccessful attempts at abortion may damage the child should be made loudly. Beck has effectively stressed that adoption and foster home resources are tragically inadequate to care for the huge supply of children involved.[11] She refers to 300,000 children in private and public agencies and 100,000 or more probably in foster homes with severe personality damage resulting, and sees this as evidence on "the salvaged but unwanted infant." That many of these children were unwanted before conception should ideally be checked by research, but even if it cannot be, the logic is fairly convincing. It is not necessary to have a cumbersome longitudinal study before putting together what data are available, with tentative conclusions, for the information of the general public.

## NOTES

1. Pohlman, E., *The Psychology of Birth Planning* (Cambridge, Mass.: Schenkman, 1969), pp. xiv, 496; "Results of unwanted conceptions: some hypotheses up for adoption," *Eugenics Quarterly*, 12:11–18 (March 1965); " 'Wanted' and 'unwanted': Toward less ambiguous definition," *Eugenics Quarterly*, 12:19–27 (March 1965); "Unwanted conceptions: research on undesirable consequences," *Eugenics Quarterly*, 14:143–154 (June 1967).

2. Lewis-Faning, E., *Family Limitation and Its Influence on Human Fertility during the Past Fifty years*. Papers of the Royal Commission, vol. 1 (London: H.M. Stationery Office, 1949), pp. 172–173.

3. Forssman, H., and Thuwe, I., "One hundred and twenty children born after application for therapeutic abortion refused," *Acta Psychiatrica Scandinavica*, 42:71–88 (1966).

4. Thompson, W. R.; Watson, J.; and Charlesworth, W. R., "The effects of prenatal maternal stress on offspring behavior in rats," *Psychological Monographs*, 76, no. 38, Whole No. 557; Montagu, M. F. A., *Prenatal influences* (Springfield, Ill.: Thomas, 1962), pp. xii, 614; Sontag, L. W., "Effect of maternal emotions in fetal developments," *Psychosomatic Obstetrics, Gynecology, and Endocrinology* (Springfield, Ill.: Thomas, 1962), pp. 8–13.

5. Pohlman, "Results of unwanted conceptions," pp. 11–18.

6. Pohlman, E., "Changes from rejection to acceptance of pregnancy," *Social Science and Medicine*, 2:333–340, 1968.

7. Westoff, C. F.; Potter, R. G.; and Sagi, P. C., *The Third Child: A Study in the Prediction of Fertility* (Princeton, N. J.: Princeton University Press, 1963), pp. 1–293.

8. Pohlman, *Psychology of Birth Planning*, pp. xiv, 496; "Unwanted conceptions," *Eugenics Quarterly*, pp. 11–18.

9. Forssman and Thuwe, "One hundred and twenty children born after abortion refusal," pp. 71–88.

10. David, H. P., *Transnational Research in Family Planning.* Progress Report No. 3 (Washington, D.C.: American Institutes for Research, 1969) (mimeographed).

11. Beck, M. B., "Abortion: the mental health consequences of unwantedness," *Seminars in Psychiatry*, 2:263–274 (August 1970).

# Discussion

**Widmann:** I think there is important information in the routine psychiatric history, which, when studied retrospectively, can provide clues for future behavior. Moreover, there is a difference between the wish to be pregnant and the wish to have a child, a very important distinction, which should be carefully assessed.

Another point, often overlooked, is the importance to the patient of sharing responsibility for the decision to have an abortion. This has something to do with the outcome for her and for the significant others in her life. The patient also wants the feeling that the doctor is involved in the decision-making process and may, in fact, be put off if the alternatives are not adequately explored in the interview. The patient, quite properly, expects to share the responsibility for the decision. Sometimes, we fail to recognize that some women want to become pregnant without anticipating that at the end of the pregnancy there will be a child they will have to take care of.

Increasingly, we are asked whether a routine psychiatric consultation is necessary for every patient applying for an abortion. I don't think it is any more essential than for any other surgical procedure. But the question raised by some gynecologists is "how do we know which patient should have the consultation and which patient should not?" For that reason, I would suggest that those of us who are still involved in obligatory consultations help formulate the criteria that may serve as guidelines to the gynecologist. For a time and experimentally, it may have some value to have routine consultations with interested gynecologists and their patients so that they may phrase guidelines for their own colleagues. In this way, our nonpsychiatrically trained colleagues will be helped to distinguish which patients they wish to refer for consultation. In North Carolina, my gynecological colleagues have drawn up a questionnaire which I use as an auxiliary in taking histories and which I hope can be developed into an instrument for predictability tests as to the types of women applying for abortions who are likely to present psychiatric problems and for whom some form of specialized help may be required. Time now spent on routine psychiatric consultations might then be utilized to better advantage by freeing more hours for essential therapeutic purposes.

**Asher:** I would like to ask Dr. Wolf what his impressions are about the historical basis for the involvement of psychiatry in abortion.

**Wolf:** I think the relationship is an ambivalent one. A great many legal reforms and much of the early agitation in terms of a humanistic approach to the liberalization of abortion laws had been encouraged by psychiatrists. Once these changes were being implemented, they seemed to have become uncertain about their continuing role.

**Widmann:** The problem lies in part with medical education which traditionally trains us that the patient is solely the woman sitting before us in the chair and not the child to be born. The concept of the traditional patient should be changed from the pregnant woman to the larger family unit for which she assumes a very large share of the nurturing responsibility.

**Cushner:** Until the concepts of psychosomatic medicine had an input into obstetrics and gynecology and medical education, the message was not driven home that uterine suspensions do not cure headaches. The Obstetrics-Gynecology Department at The Johns Hopkins Hospital includes a social anthropologist, a psychiatrist, a psychologist, and an obstetrician-gynecologist, and we look upon the patient as a woman with a uterus, who is a member of a family, lives in a neighborhood, and has various sociocultural characteristics.

**Pohlman:** I would like an example of the kind of a patient who is not ambivalent but really wants an abortion, but who, in psychiatric opinion, should not have one. Then, I should like to have a comment on the implications for the child who is born into this sort of setting.

**Brody:** An example is a woman who comes in seemingly with an unambivalent wish to be aborted which, upon interview, turns out to be an unconscious attempt on her part to punish her husband. This is the kind of problem that we would get at more frequently if we included the entire family in the research procedure.

**Beck:** How about the woman who wants an abortion, is refused, and has the baby which she must release for adoption. What kind of guilt may she have the rest of her life, wondering but never knowing what the outcome is for that child? We continue to believe that foster care is readily available, yet for the babies who need it most, it is virtually nonexistent. The Child Welfare League and the Children's Bureau can cite the figures of the huge numbers of children who are currently awaiting placement in foster care or adoption for unbelievably extended periods but for whom no resources are in sight. It should be possible, it seems to me, to study records of agencies, including social agencies, well-baby wards of hospitals, "temporary" shelters, courts, and the like, and learn about what happens to the child who is born to a mother who does not want him. We ought also to know whether she tried to have an abortion and what she actually attempted to do to terminate the pregnancy. Furthermore, efforts should be made to learn about the quality of life that the mother is capable of providing for a child she does not want but is forced to bear and rear.

**Markush:** It is very important that priorities be ordered.

We need to know more about our research goals and how to measure them. We have mentioned some of them. Family planning is one and population control is another. Good mental, physical, and social health of the child and the mother are others.

The definition of unwantedness is still closely related to the resources that the woman has. She may not want the child but she may have many resources available to her so that, for her, bearing an unwanted child may really not make much difference. If the woman has a maid or if society helps her, she and the child may fare reasonably well. But if society does not want the child, and she doesn't want him, the outcome may be very different. I think adaptability of the woman is an extremely important variable.

Since it is very difficult to do an ideal random study, we might try to take advantage of some of the natural experimental areas that are provided by different states with different laws. We might try to do some studies in contrasting cities where, for example, laws are quite liberal, versus other cities where they are not. Obviously, two populations can never be completely identical, but one can study the problem of what the outcomes might be in an area where abortion is more or less available compared with another where it is not.

# SECTION III
## ABORTION AND FAMILY PLANNING

# Abortion and Fertility Regulation in the Socialist Countries of Central and Eastern Europe*

Henry P. David, Ph.D. and
Nancy F. Russo, Ph.D.†

THIS PAPER summarizes some of the information on current trends in family planning and on contraceptive practices and legal abortions, contained in a monograph on *Family Planning and Abortion in the Socialist Countries of Central and Eastern Europe,* prepared in cooperation with country specialists.[1]

### BACKGROUND

The socialist countries of central and eastern Europe do not constitute a demographic entity. Considerable differences exist in social and economic development, urbanization, living standards, social habits, religion, and other character-

* Note: Much of the material cited in this report is based on data gathered under Contract NIH 69-2016 with the Center for Population Research of the National Institute of Child Health and Human Development.

† Associate Director and Associate Research Scientist, International Research Institute, American Institutes for Research, Washington, D.C.

istics, all of which have influenced and continue to influence population trends in varying degrees. Since the end of World War II, these countries have shared a common social and economic system inducing extensive changes, including industrialization of previously primarily agricultural economies. Rapid industrialization has produced major internal migrations from rural areas into cities and towns, and stimulated great social and occupational mobility. A large percentage of women have entered the labor force, especially in the urban areas, resulting in significant changes in family structure and in life patterns.

The demographic consequences of more than two decades of planned changes are of major proportions, including a marked decline in both fertility and mortality. However, the extent and nature of these changes differ from country to country, reflecting prevailing socioeconomic circumstances and cultural and historical traditions. Each of the socialist countries of central and eastern Europe has its own unique features,[2] and their comparison provides a rare opportunity for cross-cultural research on the effects of liberalization of abortion laws.

## TRENDS ASSOCIATED WITH LEGALIZED ABORTION

### OVERVIEW

Following the lead of the Soviet Union in 1955, liberal abortion laws were promulgated in Bulgaria and Poland (April 1956), in Hungary (June 1956), in Rumania (September 1956), in Czechoslovakia (December 1957), and Yugoslavia (February 1960). In March 1965, permissive interpretations were added to the 1950 law of the German Democratic Republic. In 1966, Romania, and, in 1967, Bulgaria revised their liberal statutes and reinstituted restrictive laws. The only country of eastern Europe now prohibiting abortion is Albania. The year legislation on abortion was enacted and the trend in birth rates are shown in Table 1 for the countries of eastern Europe.

The extent to which a woman has a legal right to determine the fate of her pregnancy is differently interpreted in the different countries. Only in Hungary and the Soviet Union is abortion available on request during the first trimester of pregnancy, provided the woman had no previous abortions during the immediately preceding twelve months. Czechoslovakia, Poland, Yugoslavia, and, to a degree, Bulgaria tend to be permissive in authorizing abortion if the pregnant woman persists in her request. Romania has moved toward more restrictive legislation but is still more liberal than most of the countries of western Europe.

The sharp rise in total registered abortions since 1957, and the concurrent decline in birth rates are shown in Table 2. The downtrend in live birth rates during the period 1948–68 shown in Table 1 suggests that the decline in birth rates was accelerated by the legalization of induced abortion. Of particular importance is the difference between total registered abortions and induced abortions, usually labeled "other abortions," including both spontaneous and illegal abortions, which tends to fluctuate with permissive or restrictive interpretations of prevailing legislation.

COUNTRY NOTES

As shown in Table 1, liberalization of abortion laws has been associated with decreasing birth rates. Even in those countries where fertility was low before abortion was legalized; i.e., Bulgaria, Czechoslovakia, and Hungary, the number of births began to decrease at a faster rate. On the other hand, in countries with higher fertility (Poland, the Soviet Union, and Yugoslavia), the decline in fertility started later and, with the exception of Poland, the rate of decline was slightly lower. It can be seen that the rate of fertility reduction has varied from country to country.

In the case of the Soviet Union and Yugoslavia, reported

TABLE 1.

LIVE BIRTH RATES PER 1,000 POPULATION IN THE SOCIALIST
COUNTRIES OF CENTRAL AND EASTERN EUROPE, 1948–1969*

| Year | Albania | Bulgaria | CSSR | GDR | Hungary | Poland | Romania | USSR | Yugoslavia |
|---|---|---|---|---|---|---|---|---|---|
| 1948 |      | 24.6  | 23.4  | 13.0  | 21.0  | 29.3  | 23.9  |       | 28.1 |
| 1949 | 39.1 | 24.7  | 22.4  | 14.8  | 20.6  | 29.5  | 27.6  |       | 30.0 |
| 1950 | 38.9 | 25.1  | 23.3  | 16.9‡ | 21.0  | 30.7  | 26.2  | 26.5  | 30.2 |
| 1951 | 38.5 | 21.0  | 22.8  | 17.4  | 20.2  | 31.0  | 25.1  | 26.8  | 27.0 |
| 1952 | 35.2 | 21.1  | 22.8  | 17.1  | 19.6  | 30.2  | 24.8  | 26.4  | 29.7 |
| 1953 | 40.9 | 20.7  | 21.2  | 16.8  | 21.6  | 29.7  | 23.8  | 24.9  | 28.4 |
| 1954 | 40.8 | 20.2  | 20.6  | 16.6  | 23.0  | 29.1  | 24.8  | 26.6  | 28.5 |
| 1955 | 44.5 | 20.1  | 20.3  | 16.7  | 21.4  | 29.1  | 25.6  | 25.7† | 26.8 |
| 1956 | 41.9 | 19.5† | 19.8  | 16.2  | 19.5† | 28.0† | 24.2† | 25.2  | 25.9 |
| 1957 | 39.1 | 18.4  | 18.9† | 15.9  | 17.0  | 27.6  | 22.9  | 25.4  | 23.7 |
| 1958 | 41.8 | 17.9  | 17.4  | 15.6  | 16.0  | 26.3  | 21.6  | 25.3  | 24.0 |
| 1959 | 41.9 | 17.6  | 16.0  | 16.9  | 15.2  | 24.7  | 20.2  | 25.0  | 23.3 |
| 1960 | 43.3 | 17.8  | 15.9  | 17.0  | 14.7  | 22.6  | 19.1  | 24.9  | 23.5† |
| 1961 | 41.2 | 17.4  | 15.8  | 17.6  | 14.0  | 20.9  | 17.5  | 23.8  | 22.7 |
| 1962 | 39.3 | 16.7  | 15.7  | 17.4  | 12.9  | 19.6  | 16.2  | 22.4  | 21.9 |
| 1963 | 39.1 | 16.4  | 16.9  | 17.6  | 13.1  | 19.0  | 15.7  | 21.2  | 21.4 |
| 1964 | 37.8 | 16.1  | 17.2  | 17.2  | 13.0  | 18.1  | 15.2  | 19.7  | 20.8 |
| 1965 | 35.2 | 15.3  | 16.4  | 16.5† | 13.1  | 17.4  | 14.6  | 18.4  | 20.9 |
| 1966 | 34.0 | 14.9  | 15.6  | 15.8  | 13.6  | 16.7  | 14.3‡ | 18.2  | 20.3 |
| 1967 | 34.0 | 15.0‡ | 15.1  | 14.8  | 14.6  | 16.3  | 27.3  | 17.4  | 19.6 |
| 1968 | 35.6 | 17.0  | 14.9  | 14.3  | 15.1  | 16.3  | 26.7  | 17.3  | 18.9 |
| 1969 | NA   | 16.9  | 15.5  | NA    | 15.0  | 16.3  | 23.3  | NA    | 18.8 |

* Based on Klinger (1969), U.N. sources, and country consultants.
† Year in which abortion law was liberalized.
‡ Year in which abortion was restricted.
NA–Not available.

national statistical averages mask the impact of induced abortion on fertility reduction. In both countries there are vast regional differences in birth rates and abortion rates.

Liberalization of abortion laws in 1956 speeded the drop in the already declining birth rate in Romania. By 1965 there were four abortions for every live birth, the highest ratio of abortions to births ever recorded. By October 1966, restrictive legislation, coupled with increases in family allowances, taxes on childless adults, prolonged divorce procedures, and halting of official importation of contraceptive pills and intrauterine devices produced a dramatic rise in the birth rate—from 12.8 per 1,000 population in December 1966 to 39.9 in September 1967. By December 1968, the birth rate had dropped to 21.5 per 1,000, probably through use of traditional contraceptive methods, clandestine purchase of modern contraceptives, resort to illegal abortions, and reduced probability of conception for a period of time after childbirth.

The German Democratic Republic offers another potential case study of the effect of changes in governmental policy, except that the impact of the tighter abortion policy in 1950 is clouded by the considerable emigration of women of childbearing age. Not enough data have been published to assess the more liberal 1965 interpretation of the statutes on termination of pregnancy. But the abortion rate is relatively low.

In Hungary, rising annual numbers of abortions, accompanied by a slowly falling birth rate, suggest to some observers that a considerable proportion of induced abortions would have been illegal, if the law had not been changed.[3] Use of the pill and the intrauterine coil is still too limited to permit adequate assessment of changes in what has been reported as ineffective contraceptive practice in Hungary.[4]

Poland, with the oldest government-supported family planning program in eastern Europe, is also the only one with both a declining birth rate and a gradual drop in the total number of abortions, which peaked in 1962. There has, however, been a rise in the abortion ratio per 100 live births—from

## TABLE 2.

### ABORTIONS AND BIRTH RATES IN SELECTED COUNTRIES OF CENTRAL AND EASTERN EUROPE, 1957–1969[1]

| Country | 1957 | 1958 | 1959 | 1960 | 1961 | 1962 | 1963 | 1964 | 1965 | 1966 | 1967 | 1968 | 1969xx |
|---|---|---|---|---|---|---|---|---|---|---|---|---|---|
| **Total Registered Abortions (in thousands)** | | | | | | | | | | | | | |
| Bulgaria | 46.2 | 55.5 | 63.8 | 74.1 | 88.7 | 97.8 | 103.8 | 112.3 | 116.0 | 119.5 | 120.4 | 109.0 | |
| CSSR | 37.5 | 89.1 | 105.5 | 114.6 | 120.3 | 115.9 | 99.3 | 90.2 | 105.8 | 115.8 | 121.2 | 124.1 | 126.9 |
| Hungary | 168.8 | 183.0 | 187.7 | 196.0 | 203.7 | 197.6 | 207.9 | 218.7 | 214.0 | 220.4 | 222.4 | 234.8 | 238.3 |
| Poland[2] | 121.8 | 126.4 | 161.5 | 233.3 | 229.5 | 271.8 | 260.3 | 246.8 | 234.6 | 222.2 | | 155.0 | |
| Yugoslavia | | | 111.8 | 133.3 | 164.5 | 200.0x | 215.0x | 227.6x | 245.4x | 265.2x | 276.2x | | |
| (Slovenia) | 7.7 | 10.6 | 11.7 | 13.7 | 14.8 | 15.1 | 15.5 | 15.4 | 16.0 | 14.8 | | | |
| Romania | | 129.0 | 235.8 | | | | | | | | | | |
| GDR | | | | | | | | 44.1 | | | | | |
| **Legalized Induced Abortions (in thousands)** | | | | | | | | | | | | | |
| Bulgaria | 30.9 | 37.5 | 45.6 | 54.8 | 68.8 | 76.7 | 83.3 | 91.5 | 96.5 | 101.4 | 93.2 | 85.2 | |
| CSSR | 7.3 | 61.4 | 79.1 | 85.3 | 94.3 | 89.8 | 70.5 | 70.7 | 79.6 | 90.3 | 96.4 | 99.9 | 102.6 |
| Hungary | 123.4 | 145.6 | 152.4 | 162.6 | 170.0 | 163.7 | 173.8 | 184.4 | 180.3 | 186.8 | 187.5 | 201.1 | 206.5 |
| Poland[2] | 36.4 | 44.2 | 79.0 | 158.0 | 155.3 | 199.4 | 190.0 | 177.5 | 168.1 | 156.7 | 146.1 | 121.7 | |
| Yugoslavia | | | 54.5 | 76.7 | 104.0 | 150.0 | 146.8 | 153.6 | 182.4 | 195.5 | 210.7 | | |
| (Slovenia) | 2.2 | 4.7 | 6.5 | 8.2 | 9.3 | 9.5 | 9.4 | 9.4 | 9.9 | 9.5 | | | |
| Romania | | 112.1 | 219.6 | | | | | | 1115.0 | | | | |
| GDR | 0.9 | 0.9 | 0.8 | 0.8 | 0.8 | 0.7 | 0.7 | 0.8 | 0.8 | 16.0x | 20.0x | | |
| **Legalized Induced Abortions per 1,000 15-49 year old females** | | | | | | | | | | | | | |
| Bulgaria | 16 | 19 | 23 | 27 | 34 | 38 | 41 | 46 | 48 | 55 | | | |
| CSSR | 2 | 19 | 25 | 28 | 29 | 28 | 22 | 22 | 24 | 27 | 28 | 28 | 28 |
| Hungary | 49 | 58 | 61 | 65 | 69 | 66 | 70 | 79 | 77 | 80 | | | |
| Poland | 5 | 6 | 11 | 21 | 20 | 24 | 21 | 20 | 20 | 18 | | | |
| Yugoslavia | | | 11 | 16 | 20 | 22 | 18 | | | | | | |
| Romania | | 26 | 51 | | | | | | 252 | | | | |

**Legalized Induced Abortions per 100 live births**

| Country | 1957 | 1958 | 1959 | 1960 | 1961 | 1962 | 1963 | 1964 | 1965 | 1966 | 1967 | 1968 | 1969xx |
|---|---|---|---|---|---|---|---|---|---|---|---|---|---|
| Bulgaria | 22 | 27 | 33 | 39 | 50 | 57 | 63 | 69 | 75 | 76 | 79 | 60 | |
| CSSR | 3 | 26 | 36 | 41 | 43 | 41 | 29 | 29 | 34 | 41 | 45 | 47 | 46 |
| Hungary | 74 | 92 | 101 | 111 | 121 | 126 | 131 | 140 | 136 | 135 | 126 | 130 | 136 |
| Poland | 5 | 6 | 11 | 24 | 25 | 33 | 33 | 32 | 42 | 42 | | | |
| Yugoslavia (Slovenia) | | 16 | 13 | 18 | 25 | 36 | 36 | 40 | 45x | 49x | 54x | | |
| Romania | 7 | 29 | 23 | 29 | 32 | 33 | 32 | 31 | 401 | 34 | | | |
| GDR | 0.4 | 0.4 | 0.4 | 0.3 | 0.3 | 0.3 | 0.3 | 0.3 | | 6 | 8 | | |

**Birth Rates per 1,000 population**

| Country | 1957 | 1958 | 1959 | 1960 | 1961 | 1962 | 1963 | 1964 | 1965 | 1966 | 1967 | 1968 | 1969xx |
|---|---|---|---|---|---|---|---|---|---|---|---|---|---|
| Albania | 39.1 | 41.8 | 41.9 | 43.3 | 41.2 | 39.3 | 39.1 | 37.8 | 35.2 | 34.0 | 34.0 | 35.6 | |
| Bulgaria | 18.4 | 17.9 | 17.6 | 17.8 | 17.4 | 16.7 | 16.4 | 16.1 | 15.3 | 14.9 | 15.0 | 17.0 | 16.9 |
| CSSR | 18.9 | 17.4 | 16.0 | 15.9 | 15.8 | 15.7 | 16.9 | 17.2 | 16.4 | 15.6 | 15.1 | 14.9 | 15.5 |
| Hungary | 17.0 | 16.0 | 15.2 | 14.7 | 14.0 | 12.9 | 13.1 | 13.0 | 13.1 | 13.6 | 14.6 | 15.1 | 15.0 |
| Poland | 27.6 | 26.3 | 24.7 | 22.6 | 20.9 | 19.6 | 19.0 | 18.1 | 17.4 | 16.7 | 16.3 | 16.3 | 16.3 |
| Yugoslavia | 23.7 | 24.0 | 23.3 | 23.5 | 22.7 | 21.9 | 21.4 | 20.8 | 20.9 | 20.3 | 19.6 | 18.9 | 18.8 |
| USSR | 25.4 | 25.3 | 25.0 | 24.9 | 23.8 | 22.4 | 21.2 | 19.7 | 18.4 | 18.2 | 17.4 | 17.3 | |
| Romania | 22.9 | 21.6 | 20.2 | 19.1 | 17.5 | 16.2 | 15.7 | 15.2 | 14.6 | 14.3 | 27.3 | 26.8 | 23.3 |
| GDR | 15.9 | 15.6 | 16.9 | 17.0 | 17.6 | 17.4 | 17.6 | 17.2 | 16.5 | 15.8 | 14.8 | 14.3 | |

1 Based on Mahlon (1970), Klinger (1967, 1969), U.N. Statistics, National Yearbooks, and country consultants.

2 Somewhat differing statistics have been reported from Poland for the years 1965–67.

CSSR = Czechoslovakia

GDR = German Democratic Republic

x = Estimate

xx = Preliminary

33 in 1962 to 42 in 1967. The major reason for the decline in fertility appears to be the intense campaign to make contraceptives widely available at very low cost. This has been accomplished without resort to restrictive legislation. The success of the contraceptive dissemination campaign in a strongly Catholic country is of special interest.

Czechoslovakia is an example of a lag in the effect of modern contraceptive practice on the abortion rate. While the rate continues to rise, stocks of locally produced pills are mounting in warehouses. Gynecologists are unable to handle the volume of requests for required examinations which must be completed before modern contraceptives can be prescribed.

## ABORTION AND FERTILITY REGULATION

While legalization of abortion seems to correlate with declining birth rates, the relationship is more complex than it appears. Women resort to abortion in different ways with differing frequency in various countries. Assessment is rendered difficult by the many intervening variables, including the changing demographic context over time (age-sex structure, age at marriage, rural-urban migration, emigration, etc.), shifting contraceptive practices resulting from introduction of the pill and the coil, the continuing conservative attitude of the medical profession, and varying socio-economic–cultural–motivational–behavioral influences. In considering the relationship between legalized abortion and birth rates, several constraints on interpretation must be noted.[5]

The reliability of statistics varies from country to country. In Czechoslovakia registration of pregnancies and abortions is carefully controlled at the district level and central collection is good. In Hungary all operations are performed in hospitals, the registration system works well, and the small size of the country facilitates accurate record keeping. Less reliance can be placed on statistics from Poland, where many women, wishing to avoid the public atmosphere of a hospital, seek out private practitioners who may make errors in registering their cases. In Yugoslavia vital statistics are published at the regional level and figures from the less developed regions of the country may not be as reliable as those from the industrial areas.[6] Registration of births and deaths is good in the German Democratic Republic; however, no statistics on abortion have been published since 1962. No national statistics are available from Albania, and little is known about Bulgarian statistics. Only scattered data have been obtained from Romania and the Soviet Union, where vast regional differences render overall figures difficult to interpret. In addition, estimates of the impact of legal abortion on birth rates requires consideration of the number of illegal abortions performed before the law was changed, and speculation on what might have happened to the illegal abortion rate if the law had not been altered.[7]

An important index is the ratio of abortions to live births in any given year. As noted in Table 2, the recorded national ratio is highest for Hungary, where abortions have exceeded births since 1959. The evidence is strong that, for a time, Romania had a much higher abortion-birth ratio than Hungary. This ratio needs to be considered, however, in the total context of abortions and the rate per 1,000 women of childbearing age, since the ratio is affected by changes both in the number of abortions and in the number of live births.

Resort to abortion is, of course, related to the effectiveness of contraceptive practice. Relative to population, abortions have been most numerous in Hungary and in Romania before 1967. The use of contraceptives is still not considered very efficient in Hungary and was virtually nonexistent in Romania. In such settings permissive legislation on abortion may reinforce contraceptive laxity. In Poland, where an active family planning association has focused on public education and the dissemination of contraceptive information, the total number of abortions and the rate per 1,000 women of childbearing age have been decreasing, while the ratio of abortions per 100 live births has continued to rise.

Tietze noted that abortion rates are usually computed per 1,000 population per year or per 1,000 women of childbearing age per year.[8] He suggests that abortion ratios also be computed per 1,000 pregnancies or per 1,000 live births. The primary effect of abortion, whether legal or illegal, induced or spontaneous, is that it increases the potential number of pregnancies in a given woman in the sense that a woman who aborts is capable of becoming pregnant again much earlier than a woman who carries her pregnancy to term. In the absence of contraception, two or three abortions may be required to replace one live birth, but, with successful contraception plus a low pregnancy rate, only slightly more than one abortion is required to replace one live birth. Thus, to evaluate the relative impact of abortion and contraception, it is necessary to estimate the number of pregnancies which would occur in the absence of contraception. The interrelationship between abortion and contraceptive practice remains to be further explored.

Scott has observed that liberalization of the abortion laws produces an increase in the gross pregnancy rate.[9] This rate indicates the number of female fetuses that would be conceived by 100 women during their reproductive lives, if a given set of age-specific pregnancy rates remained in effect. In calculating the gross pregnancy rate, it was assumed that the distribution of abortion by age of the woman would be the same as the distribution for live births. With the shift from illegal to legal abortions, the expected pattern was found in Hungary. The gross pregnancy rate rose from 146 in 1950 to 224 in 1963. Similar patterns were observed in the other countries of central and eastern Europe, except Poland. An increase in the number of abortions can be expected to produce a rise in the pregnancy rate, if the level of contraceptive practice remains low or unchanged, because of the difference in size of the "risk" population. However, improvement in contraceptive practice and effectiveness would significantly reduce such "risk."

Klinger has attempted to demonstrate the role of induced abortions in birth control by citing Hungarian data on the number of pregnancies during a woman's reproductive life.[10] By knowing how many conceptions ended in live births and how many in induced abortions in a country where abortion is available on request, it is possible to obtain an estimate of the number of potential conceptions prevented by the use of contraception. If Hungarian women during their entire reproductive life (15 to 49 years) interrupted pregnancies or were delivered of a child at the same rate as in 1967, they would bear an average of two children, while having 0.5 spontaneous abortions and 2.6 induced abortions. This means that Hungarian women, according to Klinger's calculations, would have an average of 5.1 pregnancies, half of which they would interrupt by induced abortion. Applying biological and historical studies of natural fertility, Hungarian women would be expected to have about 6.5 pregnancies during their reproductive years if no conception control were used. Based on actual Hungarian figures of 5.1 pregnancies and 2.0 births, only about 20 percent of possible pregnancies are prevented by contraceptive practice, while more than half of recorded pregnancies are terminated by induced abortion.

RESEARCH PRIORITIES

It is evident from the literature, conferences, and discussions with knowledgeable colleagues that abortion is a commonly practiced method of birth limitation throughout the world, regardless of official approval or recognition. Women resort to abortion in increasing numbers, whether as a backstop after contraceptive failure or as a refuge from laxity in contraceptive practice. Legal termination of pregnancy on request is increasingly viewed as a right of the pregnant woman. Equally evident is the lack of hard data on which to base judgments or offer policy recommendations.[11]

Much has been said and written about abortion in diverse lands where abortion may or may not have legal sanction. To the best of our knowledge, there has been no systematic attempt to organize relevant medical, behavioral, and demographic information on a global basis. We suggest that an organized effort be made under the auspices of an international consortium and in cooperation with qualified researchers in the countries concerned. What is the actual or reasonably estimated effect of legal and illegal abortion on fertility reduction under various cultural conditions? Can we agree on internationally accepted statistical procedures and/or epidemiological studies for arriving at comparable national figures? What are the costs of induced abortion in terms of needed medical manpower and facilities? What are the side effects—medical and psychosocial—of abortion, especially repeated abortion? What are the psychosocial components affecting the incidence of abortion? Can the experience gained with induced abortion in central and eastern Europe, and in Japan, be meaningfully generalized to the United States or other developed or developing countries? What questions and objections with respect to abortion are raised in various cultures and can relevant information be collected to arrive at empirical statements?

There is strong evidence from the socialist countries of central and eastern Europe that induced abortions performed in the first trimester by qualified medical personnel in hospitals entail a low risk to the life of the pregnant woman. The mortality rate in Hungary during the years 1964–67 was 1.2 per 100,000 aborted women. The chances of complications arising from induced abortions in the first trimester appear to be less than the hazards of carrying a pregnancy to term. One difficulty of recommending induced abortion as an approved procedure for developing countries—or even in the United States—is the scarcity and/or high cost of medical manpower and facilities. In the Soviet Union, where abortions are available on request, there is one physician for every 460 persons. In Chile, one of the medically more advanced countries of Latin America, there is one physician per 1,600 inhabitants. If physicians were authorized to practice abortion, and/or had the legal obligation to perform abortions on request, it is unlikely that there would be enough specialists or hospital beds to handle the demand. In the United States, the high cost of fee-oriented services already limits the access of the poor to abortion. One possible solution, especially in developing countries, is to train midwives to terminate pregnancies as well as to deliver babies. The modern vacuum-aspiration technique, imported from China via eastern Europe, plus the excellent experience with outpatient abortions in Japan, suggest that it is possible to break through the present limitations in medical manpower and hospital beds. What is needed is a medically sponsored and carefully evaluated demonstration project assessing requirements, costs, and sequelae of various techniques.

Adoption and assessment of new programs and techniques raise the question of the attitude of medical and paramedical personnel, medical institutions, and professional societies—and brings us to our third and final research suggestion. It is quite likely that, other things being equal, the acceptance of abortion by the medical profession and the conscious practice of family limitation by individuals and couples will depend, at least in part, on our ability to develop relevant behavioral research in relation to operational family planning programs.

At this moment in recorded history, our understanding of the motivational aspects of contraceptive practice and abortion is amazingly limited. Scientists concerned with the dynamics of human sexuality appear to have had little interaction with those concerned with procreative aspects, and vice versa. Even in those countries where abortion laws are permissive or abortion is condoned, the behavioral characteristics of women seeking abortions have so far received little research attention. What are the social, behavioral, and economic costs of an unwanted pregnancy to the mother, the child, and society? What motivates a woman to seek repeated abortions? What is the social effect of the attitudes of medical and paramedical personnel toward family planning and abortion?

In cooperation with demographic, psychiatric, and psychological research centers in central and eastern Europe, we are presently attempting to develop joint programs of psychosocial research in family planning and abortion-seeking behavior. A brief description of three such projects will serve as examples.

(a) In Prague, we are planning a follow-up study of 200 children born in 1961, 1962, and 1963 to women refused abortion on initial request and on subsequent appeal. These children and their mothers will be matched with children born to women who knowingly stopped some form of contraceptive practice and planned to have a child. We shall also study the fathers and, if possible, interview those women who managed not to have a child after their request for abortion was refused. One objective is to learn more about the impact of "unwantedness" on the child, the family, and society.

(b) In Budapest, we are proposing to study psychosocial aspects of repeated abortion-seeking behavior in situations where contraceptives are readily available. Two groups of women will be studied. All will have received instructions in contraception after the first abortion. One group will have had at least two additional abortions after the initial abortion, while the second group of women will have had no further conceptions. One objective will be to learn more about substituting effective contraceptive practice for abortion as a preferred method of birth limitation.

(c) In Yugoslavia, a draft proposal is being developed for a study of attitudes toward family planning and abortion among physicians, nurses, midwives, and other "gatekeeper" personnel. This will be a cross-sectional effort with selected samples taken during training, immediately on completion of training, one year after completion of training and, five, ten, and fifteen years after completion of training, etc. It is hoped that the results of this study will provide additional information about educating and/or "influencing" a key group of opinion makers.

A major assumption of the evolving cooperative program in

transnational family planning research is the importance of psychosocial correlates of fertility, family planning, and abortion. There is an expectation that better understanding of the motivational context of family planning behavior is likely to yield fresh insights for the development of educational materials aimed at specific target populations, improvements of local operational service programs, and a basis for the acquisition of new knowledge.

CONCLUSION

World-wide, the dynamics of family planning have proved to be far more complex than the processes of reducing mortality. Freedom to determine the number and spacing of children is proclaimed as a fundamental human right by men and women of diverse persuasions, including Americans who are petitioning their state governments for liberalization of abortion legislation. Differences in ideology should not deter utilization of experience abroad or joining with colleagues in other lands in studying social and behavioral components of all aspects of family planning, including abortion. Learning from diverse successes and failures is certain to enhance progress toward joint solutions of the urgent problems facing mankind.

## NOTES

1. David, H. P., *Family Planning and Abortion in the Socialist Countries of Central and Eastern Europe* (New York: The Population Council, 1970), pp. 1–306.

2. Vukovich, G., "Fertility differentials in Eastern and Central European socialist countries." Paper presented at the Conference of the International Union for the Scientific Study of Population (London, September 1969).

3. Peel, J., and Potts, M., *Textbook of Contraceptive Practice* (Cambridge: University Press, 1969), pp. 1–296.

4. Szabady, E., "Family planning trends: The Hungarian Study." *Demográfia*, 11:333–346 (1968).

5. Frederikson, H., and Brackett, J. W., "Demographic effects of abortion," *Public Health Reports*, 83:999–1010 (December 1968).

6. Potts, M., "Legal abortion in Eastern Europe," *Eugenics Review*, 59:232–250 (December 1967).

7. *Ibid.*

8. Tietze, C., Personal communication.

9. Scott, M., *Projections of the Populations of the Communist Countries of Eastern Europe, by Age and Sex: 1965–1985*, International Population Reports, P-91, No. 14 (Washington: U. S. Government Printing Office, 1965).

10. Klinger, A., "Demographic aspects of abortion." Paper presented at Conference of the International Union for the Scientific Study of Population (London, September 1969).

11. Beck, M. B.; Newman, S. H.; and Lewit, S., "Abortion: A national public and mental health problem—past, present, and proposed research," *American Journal of Public Health*, 59:2131–2143 (December 1969).

# Demographic Consequences of Legal Abortion

James W. Brackett, B.A.*

THAT induced abortion was used to regulate human fertility almost from the dawn of human existence is an axiom among population experts. In more recent times, most societies attempted to restrict the practice of abortion, partly on religious and moral grounds, but undoubtedly largely because the primitive methods available until relatively recently resulted in the death or maiming of large numbers of women. Despite often severe penalties on abortionists and aborted women alike and the high risk of illness and death, abortion continued to be employed.

With the evolution of medical science, safter methods of abortion emerged, thus removing one of the principal bases for restricting abortion. Changing religious and moral views, coupled with the realization in many societies that illegal abortion—using primitive and dangerous methods—is widespread, led some countries to liberalize their abortion laws. Although less often stated, it is likely that concern over high birth rates also played a role in the decision of some countries.

The Soviet Union was the first country to provide abortion

* Chief, Analysis and Evaluation Division, Office of Population, Technical Assistance Bureau, Agency for International Development, Washington, D.C.

virtually on request. In 1920, Lenin's new government made abortion legally obtainable free of charge. In an effort to curtail the morbid consequences of illegal abortion—which allegedly resulted in illness in 50 percent of the women and death in 4 percent—the decree specified that only physicians could perform abortions. The new law was justified under Lenin's principle that one of the basic rights of a citizen is that of deciding whether her child should be born.[1]

A detailed analysis of the demographic consequences of this law is not possible because statistics on births and abortions are inadequate and because a series of major upheavals complicates interpretation of whatever information is at hand. However, available data for Moscow, where the abortion rate rose from 19 per 100 live births in 1921, to 55 in 1926, and to 270 in 1934,[2] indicate that abortions increased very sharply. By 1935 the problem had become so acute that the Soviet government placed certain limitations on abortion, and in 1936 abortions were further restricted—essentially to medical grounds.

The Soviet Union once again liberalized its abortion laws in 1955, but again it is not possible to analyze the consequences. Abortion statistics have not been published. In fact, some Soviet demographers and public health people maintain that abortion statistics are not collected. This assertion was repeated to the author on his visit to the Soviet Union in September 1969. Other reports indicate that abortion data are indeed collected. Given the Soviet Union's preoccupation with record keeping, it is inconceivable that abortions would fail to be recorded.

Mehlan gives some data on abortions in the Soviet Union, the origins of which are not documented in his manuscript.[3] He speaks of a threefold increase in the number of legal abortions between 1955 (the year of legalization) and 1963. He further states that the largest increase occurred immediately after liberalization and that since 1965 there has been a slight decline. He estimates the number of abortions in the Soviet Union at 6 million per year. Since there are currently fewer than four million births in that country, his figures imply that three pregnancies out of five are aborted. He attributes to the Soviet writer, Sadvokasova, a statement that three out of four pregnancies in the Russian Republic are aborted. These data require careful evaluation and analysis.

## EFFECT ON ILLEGAL ABORTION

Most eastern European countries liberalized their abortion laws in the mid-1950s, following the lead of the Soviet Union. East Germany experimented briefly with liberalized abortion in the late 1940s, but did not follow the Soviet lead after 1955.

The East German experience is interesting from the standpoint of the effect of liberalized legal abortion on illegal abortion. On the basis of data for 7,000 women of childbearing age who were interviewed by physicians in private practice, Mehlan reports that both legal and illegal abortions increased when social indications for abortion were adopted.[4] He attributes the rise in illegal abortion to changing attitudes toward abortion.

However, the East German experience may not be typical because of the difficult circumstances that prevailed in postwar Germany. During the late 1940s, large numbers of Germans were forced out of lost German territories and other parts of Europe to find residence in the rubble of postwar Germany. Many women had lost their husbands or prospective husbands in the war and were seeking to make a life for themselves from what was left. The country was under military occupation. Illegitimacy was exceptionally high. Such circumstances are likely to produce atypical results.

Available data for other eastern European countries show divergent patterns following liberalization of abortion laws. Data on hospital admissions for "other" abortions—that is, illegal plus spontaneous abortions—covering the period prior to and after liberalization are available for Bulgaria, Czechoslovakia, Hungary, and Poland (Table 1). Data on illegal and spontaneous abortions separately are not available. "Other"

TABLE 1.

OUTCOMES OF REPORTED PREGNANCIES IN CZECHOSLOVAKIA, HUNGARY, JAPAN, AND POLAND

| Country and year | Numbers (in thousands) | | | | Percent of total pregnancies | | |
|---|---|---|---|---|---|---|---|
| | Pregnancies[1] | Births | Legal abortions | Other abortions | Births | Legal abortions | Other abortions |
| Czechoslovakia | | | | | | | |
| 1953 ... | 303 | 272 | 2 | 29 | 89.8 | .7 | 9.6 |
| 1954 ... | 301 | 267 | 3 | 31 | 88.7 | 1.0 | 10.3 |
| 1955 ... | 300 | 265 | 2 | 33 | 88.3 | .7 | 11.0 |
| 1956 ... | 296 | 262 | 3 | 31 | 88.5 | 1.0 | 10.5 |
| 1957[3] .. | 290 | 253 | 7 | 30 | 87.2 | 2.4 | 10.3 |
| 1958 ... | 324 | 235 | 61 | 28 | 72.5 | 18.8 | 8.6 |
| 1959 ... | 322 | 217 | 79 | 26 | 67.4 | 24.5 | 8.1 |
| 1960 ... | 331 | 217 | 88 | 26 | 65.6 | 26.6 | 7.9 |
| 1961 ... | 338 | 218 | 94 | 26 | 64.5 | 27.8 | 7.7 |
| 1962 ... | 333 | 217 | 90 | 26 | 65.2 | 27.0 | 7.8 |
| 1963 ... | 336 | 236 | 71 | 29 | 70.2 | 21.1 | 8.6 |
| 1964 ... | 341 | 241 | 71 | 29 | 70.7 | 20.8 | 8.5 |
| 1965 ... | 338 | 232 | 80 | 26 | 68.6 | 23.7 | 7.7 |
| 1966 ... | 339 | 223 | 90 | 26 | 65.8 | 26.5 | 7.7 |
| 1967 ... | 337 | 216 | 96 | 25 | 64.1 | 28.5 | 7.4 |
| Hungary | | | | | | | |
| 1950 ... | 232 | 196 | 2 | 34 | 84.5 | .7 | 14.6 |
| 1951 ... | 229 | 191 | 2 | 36 | 83.4 | .9 | 15.7 |
| 1952 ... | 230 | 186 | 2 | 42 | 80.9 | .9 | 18.3 |
| 1953 ... | 250 | 207 | 3 | 40 | 82.8 | 1.2 | 16.0 |
| 1954 ... | 281 | 223 | 16 | 42 | 79.4 | 5.7 | 14.9 |
| 1955 ... | 288 | 210 | 35 | 43 | 72.9 | 12.2 | 14.9 |
| 1956[3] .. | 317 | 193 | 83 | 41 | 60.0 | 26.2 | 12.9 |
| 1957 ... | 330 | 167 | 123 | 40 | 50.6 | 37.3 | 12.1 |
| 1958 ... | 341 | 158 | 146 | 37 | 46.3 | 42.8 | 10.9 |
| 1959 ... | 338 | 151 | 152 | 35 | 44.7 | 45.0 | 10.4 |
| 1960 ... | 342 | 146 | 162 | 34 | 42.7 | 47.4 | 9.9 |
| 1961 ... | 344 | 140 | 170 | 34 | 40.7 | 49.4 | 9.9 |
| 1962 ... | 328 | 130 | 164 | 34 | 39.6 | 50.0 | 10.4 |
| 1963 ... | 340 | 132 | 174 | 34 | 38.8 | 51.1 | 10.0 |
| 1964 ... | 350 | 132 | 184 | 34 | 37.7 | 52.6 | 9.7 |
| 1965 ... | 347 | 133 | 180 | 34 | 38.3 | 51.9 | 9.8 |
| 1966 ... | 359 | 138 | 187 | 34 | 38.4 | 52.1 | 9.5 |
| 1967 ... | 372 | 149 | 188 | 35 | 40.1 | 50.5 | 9.4 |

Source: Data for eastern European countries, Paul F. Myers, *Demographic Trends in Eastern Europe* (Joint Economic Committee of the U.S. Congress, 1970). Data for Japan from "Selected statistics concerning fertility regulations in Japan" Institute of Population Problems, Research Series, No. 181, December 15, 1967.

TABLE 1.

OUTCOMES OF REPORTED PREGNANCIES IN CZECHOSLOVAKIA,
HUNGARY, JAPAN, AND POLAND *(con'd)*

| Country and year | Preg-nan-cies[1] | Births | Legal abor-tions | Other abor-tions | Births | Legal abor-tions | Other abor-tions |
|---|---|---|---|---|---|---|---|
| | Numbers (in thousands) | | | | Percent of total pregnancies | | |
| Japan[2] | | | | | | | |
| 1950 ... | 2,827 | 2,338 | 489 | ... | 82.7 | 17.3 | ... |
| 1951 ... | 2,776 | 2,138 | 638 | ... | 77.0 | 23.0 | ... |
| 1952[3] .. | 2,811 | 2,005 | 806 | ... | 71.3 | 28.7 | ... |
| 1953 ... | 2,936 | 1,868 | 1,068 | ... | 63.6 | 36.4 | ... |
| 1954 ... | 2,913 | 1,770 | 1,143 | ... | 60.8 | 39.2 | ... |
| 1955 ... | 2,901 | 1,731 | 1,170 | ... | 59.7 | 40.3 | ... |
| 1956 ... | 2,824 | 1,665 | 1,159 | ... | 59.0 | 41.0 | ... |
| 1957 ... | 2,689 | 1,567 | 1,122 | ... | 58.3 | 41.7 | ... |
| 1958 ... | 2,781 | 1,653 | 1,128 | ... | 59.4 | 40.6 | ... |
| 1959 ... | 2,725 | 1,626 | 1,099 | ... | 59.7 | 40.3 | ... |
| 1960 ... | 2,669 | 1,606 | 1,063 | ... | 60.2 | 39.8 | ... |
| 1961 ... | 2,625 | 1,590 | 1,035 | ... | 60.6 | 39.4 | ... |
| 1962 ... | 2,604 | 1,619 | 985 | ... | 62.2 | 37.8 | ... |
| 1963 ... | 2,615 | 1,660 | 955 | ... | 63.5 | 36.5 | ... |
| 1964 ... | 2,596 | 1,717 | 879 | ... | 66.1 | 33.9 | ... |
| 1965 ... | 2,667 | 1,824 | 843 | ... | 68.4 | 31.6 | ... |
| 1966 ... | 2,167 | 1,359 | 808 | ... | 62.7 | 37.3 | ... |
| 1967 ... | 2,679 | 1,932 | 747 | ... | 72.1 | 27.9 | ... |
| Poland | | | | | | | |
| 1955 ... | 897 | 794 | 1 | 102 | 88.5 | .1 | 11.4 |
| 1956[3] .. | 901 | 780 | 19 | 102 | 86.6 | 2.1 | 11.3 |
| 1957 ... | 903 | 782 | 36 | 85 | 86.6 | 4.0 | 9.4 |
| 1958 ... | 881 | 755 | 44 | 82 | 85.7 | 5.0 | 9.3 |
| 1959 ... | 885 | 723 | 79 | 83 | 81.7 | 8.9 | 9.4 |
| 1960 ... | 902 | 669 | 158 | 75 | 74.2 | 17.5 | 8.3 |
| 1961 ... | 857 | 628 | 155 | 74 | 73.3 | 18.1 | 8.6 |
| 1962 ... | 871 | 600 | 199 | 72 | 68.9 | 22.8 | 8.3 |
| 1963 ... | 848 | 588 | 190 | 70 | 69.3 | 22.4 | 8.3 |
| 1964 ... | 808 | 563 | 176 | 69 | 69.7 | 21.8 | 8.5 |
| 1965 ... | 781 | 546 | 168 | 67 | 69.9 | 21.5 | 8.6 |
| 1966 ... | 753 | 530 | 157 | 66 | 70.4 | 20.8 | 8.8 |

[1] "Pregnancies" are the sum of the outcomes of pregnancy for which data are given in the table. No allowance was made for stillbirths, ectopic pregnancies, missed abortions, etc., which would have increased the number of pregnancies, or for multiple births, which would have decreased the number of pregnancies.

[2] Excludes "other" abortions, which are spontaneous and illegally induced abortions. Data are given for legally induced abortions only.

[3] Abortion law liberalized.

abortions in Bulgaria are shown as increasing somewhat, while data for Czechoslovakia, Hungary, and Poland show declines.

Interpretations are complicated by a series of factors. Following liberalization, the total number of pregnancies increased sharply, reflecting a sharp rise in the number of legal abortions. The effect was a major reduction in the *average* number of months a woman remains pregnant per pregnancy, but, at least on the basis of reported pregnancies, little change in the *total* number of months the average woman remains pregnant. Thus, there was a sharp increase in the number of early pregnancy months when the chance of spontaneous abortion is at its peak. Furthermore, nonviable terminations of late pregnancies are classified as stillbirths rather than as abortions.

If the above logic is correct, the introduction of large-scale legal abortion could result in an increase in the number of spontaneous abortions. Since for eastern European countries, spontaneous and illegal abortions are grouped together as "other" abortions, one might assume from the reported trends of "other" abortions that illegal abortion has declined, at least in Czechoslovakia and Hungary.

Other factors have affected the abortion statistics, however, and these should be examined to determine whether they lend support to the above conclusion. Tietze reports that eastern European physicians with whom he has discussed the problem agreed that a substantially larger proportion of both illegal and spontaneous abortions are now being reported, because women no longer fear prosecution for illegal abortion and because restrictions on private medical practice force many more women into hospitals.[5] David reports that some gynecologists may hospitalize women under the pretext of spontaneous abortion to avoid charging fees for abortion on demand, or because they live outside the service area for the hospital and thus cannot be admitted for induced abortion.[6] Both Tietze and David tend to support the supposition that illegal abortions may have declined.

There are important differences between Mehlan's East German data and data for other eastern European countries that may affect our interpretations. As stated above, the East German data were obtained from interviews by physicians. In other words, women were asked for pregnancy histories. Data obtained in this manner would not be influenced by changes in medical practice or the types of errors mentioned above. They would be subject to errors of recall and to the willingness of respondents to reply truthfully to questions of an intimate nature. Presumably, women would be less inhibited when speaking with their private physicians than they would be in other interview situations, since they may fear the consequences of withholding potentially important medical information. Future research might include comparisons of data obtained from routine hospital records and data collected in in-depth interviews by physicians.

Some eastern European population and health people maintain that large numbers of unreported illegal abortions were performed prior to liberalization. For example, an annual figure of 100,000 is mentioned for Hungary for the early 1950s. There is little doubt that illegal abortions were numerous prior to liberalization, but the figure of 100,000 seems to be more supposition than hard fact. Moreover, there has been a general attempt to show that the large increase in legal abortion was merely the transfer of illegal abortion from the back room to the hospital.

## EFFECT ON BIRTHS

In the six eastern European countries with liberal abortion laws, birth rates for the region as a whole declined by 40 percent between the early 1950s and the mid-1960s. The Soviet Union's birth rate declined by about one-third during the same period, while Japan's birth rate dropped by about one-half between the late 1940s, when abortion was liberalized, and the mid-1960s.

That the legalization of abortion played a significant role in this decline cannot be denied. However, it would not be correct to attribute all of the decline to abortion. Moreover, it is important to remember that the act of liberalization merely provided the method for fertility reduction. The employment of the method depended upon the free choice of individual women.

Because many of the countries in question emerged from World War II with major distortions in their population structure, we should first attempt to determine the extent to which changes in birth rates were due to changes in the age-sex structure.

For eastern Europe, Myers uses age-adjusted birth rates to conclude that most of the declines in crude birth rates were due essentially to declines in age-specific fertility.[7] He also concludes from an analysis of marriage rates that the decline in age-specific fertility is due to a decline in marital fertility and not to changes in the proportion marrying at each age.

Taeuber draws essentially the same conclusion for Japan when she states that "the explanation [for the reductions in fertility between 1947 and 1954] must be sought in the changing rate of reproduction in a mature and largely married population of women."[8]

Information for the Soviet Union is harder to interpret. The Soviet birth rate did not change very much during the decade of the 1950s but declined sharply after 1960. My earlier published explanation of this phenomenon is that the improving sex ratio in the reproductive ages offset reduction in marital fertility until about 1960. Improving sex ratios were insufficient to prevent declines after 1960 because sex ratios were already normal in the age groups producing most of the births.

By the mid-1960s another factor began to affect the Soviet birth rate, namely, the coming of age of children born during the second World War, when birth rates were sharply reduced —in some years to one-third the prewar level.

In the absence of marital fertility rates, I attempted to obtain some understanding of Soviet fertility trends by analyzing trends in estimates of the paternal gross reproduction rate. My use of this measure is based on the assumption that in the male-deficient Soviet Union the limiting factor to marriage is the supply of men. Since men throughout the period had an abundant supply of women from among whom to select mates, the proportions married at various ages would fluctuate within a much narrower range for men than for women. The paternal gross reproduction rate should therefore be a reasonable approximation of marital fertility.

This exercise suggests that marital fertility declined more rapidly during the five years preceding liberalization than during the five years immediately thereafter. Very rapid declines followed during the early 1960s. The paradox may be due to abnormally high "make-up" fertility during the first years of the 1950s as life became more settled, but clearly this is only a supposition. Estimates of the paternal gross reproduction rate could also be faulty. Because births by age of father are not reported for the Soviet Union, paternal gross reproduction rates had to be based on patterns of age-specific fertility rates for males in other countries. The actual pattern might be quite different from that assumed.

Unfortunately, we must wait until more data are released or new techniques designed to exploit those data that are available before a satisfactory understanding of Soviet fertility and the role of abortion is possible.

For Japan and the eastern European countries, it appears that declines in birth rates are due largely to declines in marital fertility, which, of course, may be realized by resorting to contraception or abortion. As Frederiksen and I concluded in an earlier paper, the availability of abortion seems to have resulted in some relaxation of contraceptive use in eastern Europe, while contraception seems to have increased and abortion decreased in Japan.[9]

Field research is required to test the validity of these con-

clusions and the reasons for the differences. Pending the results of such a study, my guess would be that the explanation
of the divergent trends lies in differences in the contraceptive
techniques used in the respective areas. Withdrawal is by far
the most widely practiced technique among eastern Euro-
peans; the condom, among the Japanese. The decision to use
withdrawal must be made at the height of sexual excitement.
Thus, since abortion is available to prevent unwanted births,
couples may be tempted to forgo its use at the moment of
truth. Condom users, on the other hand, normally make the
decision to use the device prior to initial intromission and are,
thus, relieved of the decision at the last moment.

Data from several countries in eastern Europe and from
Japan provide the basis for an analysis of the characteristics
of women using abortion.

Data for Czechoslovakia, Hungary, and Japan permit analysis of abortion by age of aborting woman. In Japan, abortion
is relied upon rather heavily by women under 20 years of age
and those over 30. In both 1960 and 1965, abortions were
performed in about 43 percent of the reported pregnancies in
women 15 to 19 years of age, in 40 percent or more of those
30 to 34 years of age, in two-thirds of the women 35 to 39 years
old, and more than 90 percent of women 45 years or older.
In contrast, between 20 and 30 percent of the pregnancies
among women age 20 to 29 were aborted. (See Table 2.)

The Hungarian pattern is one of increasing proportions
aborted with each successive age group—from 40 percent for
women age 15 to 19 to 80 percent for those 40 years or older,
in 1967.

The Czechoslovakian pattern is a modified version of the
Japanese. The proportions of women with abortions are
slightly higher among women 15 to 19 years of age than
among those 20 to 24 years of age for each of the three years
shown.

These data suggest that in all three countries abortion is
used by older women to terminate childbearing and by
younger women to postpone childbearing. Rates are suffi-

## TABLE 2.
### INDUCED ABORTION AS A PERCENT OF PREGNANCIES IN CZECHOSLOVAKIA, AND JAPAN

| Country and year | \multicolumn{7}{c}{Age of woman} |
|---|---|---|---|---|---|---|---|

| Country and year | 15–19 | 20–24 | 25–29 | 30–34 | 35–39 | 40–44 | 45–49 |
|---|---|---|---|---|---|---|---|
| **Czechoslovakia** | | | | | | | |
| Percent | | | | | | | |
| 1960 | 16.4 | 14.5 | 26.8 | 42.0 | 54.8 | 60.9 | 50.0 |
| 1964 | 13.2 | 11.5 | 20.1 | 34.3 | 49.1 | 60.0 | 25.0 |
| 1966 | 20.0 | 17.5 | 27.5 | 43.4 | 55.4 | 42.9 | 50.0 |
| Change | | | | | | | |
| 1960–64 | − 3.2 | − 3.0 | − 6.7 | − 7.7 | − 5.7 | − 0.9 | −25.0 |
| 1964–66 | + 6.8 | + 6.0 | + 7.4 | + 9.1 | + 6.3 | −17.1 | +25.0 |
| **Hungary** | | | | | | | |
| Percent | | | | | | | |
| 1960 | 28.9 | 39.1 | 54.7 | 66.2 | 71.6 | 78.6 | |
| 1964 | 43.1 | 45.8 | 58.8 | 70.5 | 78.3 | 82.4 | |
| 1967 | 40.5 | 44.0 | 56.0 | 68.2 | 78.7 | 80.0 | |
| Change | | | | | | | |
| 1960–64 | +14.2 | + 6.7 | + 4.1 | + 4.3 | + 6.7 | + 3.8 | |
| 1964–67 | − 2.6 | −1 .8 | − 2.8 | − 2.3 | + 0.4 | − 2.4 | |
| **Japan** | | | | | | | |
| Percent | | | | | | | |
| 1960 | 43.8 | 27.4 | 29.6 | 47.6 | 69.7 | 82.6 | 90.5 |
| 1965 | 43.1 | 21.7 | 21.6 | 39.3 | 66.8 | 87.6 | 92.6 |
| 1966 | 43.5 | 25.7 | 26.8 | 46.0 | 69.8 | 87.1 | 92.3 |
| Change | | | | | | | |
| 1960–65 | − 0.7 | − 5.7 | − 8.0 | − 8.3 | − 2.9 | + 5.0 | + 2.1 |
| 1965–66 | + 0.4 | + 4.0 | + 5.2 | + 6.7 | + 3.0 | − 0.5 | − 0.3 |

Sources:

Czechoslovakia: women by age group, *Statistica Rocenka,* 1966, 1968; induced abortions, *Demograficka 1967* and *Zdrovotnika Statistika,* 1966; live births, *Statistica Rocenka,* 1963, 1966, 1968.

Hungary: live births and reported induced abortions, Hungarian Central Statistical office, unpublished; women by age group, *Magyarorszag Uapesidese,* 1962, 1964; *Demografiai Evkonyv* 1967.

Japan: 1960, *Selected Statistics Concerning Fertility Regulation in Japan,* Table 13, December 15, 1967; 1965, women by age group, *Census of Japan,* 1965 Prefecture Volumes; births, Vital Statistics 1965 Japan, Vol. 1; abortions, Selected Statistics Concerning Fertility Regulation in Japan, Table 13, December 15, 1967; 1966, live births and women by age group, *Japan Statistical Yearbook 1968*; abortions, *Statistics Concerning Eugenic Protection,* Ministry of Health and Welfare, 1966.

ciently high at all ages, however, to leave little doubt that abortion is heavily relied upon to limit births.

We were able to construct estimates of age-specific pregnancy, birth, and abortion rates for 46 prefectures in Japan for 1965. Because of special data problems, a methodological note is required at this point.

Live births by age of mother, population by age and sex, and total numbers of abortions were reported for 1965 for each prefecture. Abortions by age by prefecture, however, were available only for 1967, a year for which neither births by age of mother nor population by age by prefecture were available.[10] It was necessary, therefore, to combine data for the two dates. Adjustments using the "racking" process were made in the 1967 abortion data to force them into agreement with the 1965 age distribution for abortions by age for Japan as a whole and with the total number of abortions in each prefecture for that year. The resulting numbers were then used as numerators for the calculation of age-specific abortion rates.

"Pregnancies" in Japan were assumed to be the sum of live births and legally induced abortions. This concept is, of course, less than perfect because it does not include other outcomes of pregnancies such as stillbirths, spontaneous and illegally induced abortions, ectopic pregnancies, etc. Failure to include these events is partially offset by counting each child in a multiple birth as a separate pregnancy.

Variations among prefectures were largest for the youngest age group, 15 to 19 years, in which from 18 percent to 73 percent of the pregnancies were aborted; and least for the oldest group, 45 to 49 years, in which the range was from 82 percent to 99 percent.

## CONSEQUENCES OF REIMPOSING RESTRICTIONS ON ABORTION

No paper on abortion would be complete without some mention of recent events in Romania. In October 1966, the

Romanian government decreed that, effective November 1 of that year, abortion would be available on essentially medical grounds only. Women with four or more children under their care, women 45 years old and over, cases of rape or incest, etc., were excepted.

At the same time the official importation of contraceptives was curtailed, divorce was made very difficult, and a strong program of child allowances was established.

The factor that sparked this action is not hard to find. Romania's birth rate in 1966 dropped to 14.3 while abortions reportedly exceeded one million.

The effect of the action was seen during the following spring and summer. Beginning about March 1967, the birth rate shot upward. In May, it reached 20 per 1,000; in June, 27; and by July, nearly 38. It remained in the 37 to 39 range through October and then began to decline. By the summer of 1968, the birth rate was approaching 25.

By the winter of 1968–69, the most recent period for which birth rates are reported, the rate fell a little below 25, but since Romania's birth rate has historically been low during that season, it is not possible to say whether this is a seasonal factor or a leveling off of the trend.

The Romanian population seems to have been caught off guard for a few months before regaining some measure of control over their reproduction. Many women who were already pregnant were forced to carry their babies to full term. Perhaps other couples had to learn where condoms could be obtained or get accustomed to using withdrawal. At any rate, the Romanian case deserves careful study.

## RESEARCH NEEDS

In order to carry out high quality international and cross-cultural research on abortion it is essential that abortion data be collected on a comparable and carefully defined basis. Such effort should ideally be centered in the World Health Organization or in the United Nations Statistical Office. Pending new initiatives by one or the other of these organizations, countries with liberal abortion laws should be encouraged to draw up a uniform set of concepts and to recommend items of information to be collected.

Given statistically comparable data on detailed characteristics of aborting women, women giving birth, and women in the general population, it should be possible to use the techniques of demographic analysis to gain considerable insight into the demographic consequences of abortion.

A more fundamental understanding would come from special studies of the factors motivating women to seek abortion. Such information would be quite useful in projecting future trends in abortion. Broader studies designed to determine the motivating factors for contraception as well as abortion, and the interrelationship between the two, would be even more valuable. For example, why do some women rely heavily on abortion to the exclusion of contraception? Why do other women use contraception effectively and abortion only for contraceptive failures? Why do others in societies in which abortion is legal decline to use abortion at all, even when they already have more children than they want?

Given the answers to the above questions, special programs might be focused on abortion-seeking women to demonstrate the advantages of prevention (i.e., contraception). The information could also be used in countries in which efforts are being made to curtail illegal abortion.

Other studies might focus on the impact of denied abortions on mothers and children. What is the attitude of a mother toward her child when she is denied an abortion? How does her treatment of the child differ in a society in which abortion is legal from one in which it is illegal? How does attitude and treatment differ between women who had contraceptive failures but did not seek abortion and those who did seek abortion but were turned down? Or were granted abortion? Or gave birth to a "wanted" child? What influence does the legal and social situation have on the above?

What influence do these factors have on the abortion-seeking behavior of women?

Some of these factors could be studied in eastern Europe or Japan, where abortion has been legal for about two decades. The influence of the legal status may be studied specifically in Romania where abortion has been restricted after a period in which it was legal on request. Did the factor of restriction change attitudes? Or was the sharp drop in abortion more a reflection of its inaccessability? What factors account for the sharp rise in the birth rate in Romania following restriction? What factors account for the sharp decline?

## CONCLUSION

In this paper I have discussed the impact of legal abortion on illegal abortion as well as on birth rates. Although available data are somewhat contradictory, it seems likely that legal abortion has generally resulted in a reduction of illegal abortion. There appears to be little basis for doubting that legal abortion was a prime factor in the sharp reductions in birth rates in Japan and eastern Europe since 1950.

Should other countries elect to provide abortion on similar terms, the likely result would be a sharp reduction in fertility. Ryder and Westoff reported that nearly one-third of all married couples in the United States who intended to have no more children had at least one additional child.[11] If abortion were legally available, many couples would likely resort to abortion to ensure that they do not exceed their fertility desires.

To date, the countries that have provided abortion on demand have, in general, been advanced countries with virtually total literacy and adequate medical facilities to handle abortion cases. Extending the experience of advanced countries to less-developed regions is risky. However, given the large number of illegal abortions that are performed in virtually every country, it is likely that legal abortion would be popular in less-developed nations as well. The limiting factor may be medical facilities, although current research on postconceptive, self-administrable techniques of fertility regulation may remove this limitation.

Singapore has recently liberalized its abortion law. India is currently considering similar legislation. We may thus be able to study what impact abortion can make in a less-developed country.

## NOTES

1. Brackett, J. W., "Demographic trends and population policy in the Soviet Union," *Dimensions of Soviet Economic Power,* Joint Economic Committee of the U. S. Congress (1962); Brackett, J. W. and DePauw, John W., "Population policy and demographic trends in the Soviet Union," *New Directions in the Soviet Economy,* Joint Economic Committee of the U. S. Congress (1966).

2. Lorimer, F., *The Population of the Soviet Union: History and Prospects* (Geneva: League of Nations, 1946), p. 128.

3. Mehlan, K. H., "Abortion in eastern Europe," in *Abortion in a Changing World, Volume 1* (ed. Robert E. Hall) (New York: Columbia University Press, 1970), pp. 302–314.

4. Mehlan, K. H., In *Internationale Abortsituation, Abortbekämofung, Antikonzeption* (ed. K. H. Mehlan) (Leipzig: Georg Thieme, 1961), pp. 55–60.

5. Tietze, C., "The demographic significance of legal abortion in eastern Europe," *Demography,* 1:119–125 (1964).

6. David, H., *Family Planning and Abortion in the Socialist Countries of Central and Eastern Europe* (New York: The Population Council, 1970), p. 106.

7. Myers, P. F., *Demographic Trends in Eastern Europe,* The Joint Economic Committee of the U. S. Congress (May 1970), pp. 68–148.

8. Taeuber, I., *The Population of Japan* (Princeton: Princeton University Press, 1958), p. 238.

9. Frederiksen, H., and Brackett, J. W., "Demographic effects of abortion," *Public Health Reports,* 83:999–1010 (December 1968).

10. Letter from Dr. Minoru Muramatsu of the Family Planning Federation of Japan to Mrs. Martha Bargar of the International Demographic Statistics Center, Bureau of the Census, October 1968.

11. *New York Times,* November 23, 1969.

# Induced Abortion and Family Planning: Gynecological Aspects*

Carl W. Tyler, Jr., M.D., John D. Asher, M.D., and Malcolm G. Freeman, M.D.†

RECENT recognition of induced abortion as a world-wide method of fertility control has already resulted in several efforts aimed at replacing abortion with modern methods of contraception. Our purpose in this review is to discuss abortion in two countries where it is a major mode of fertility control and to examine the effectiveness of five abortion control programs in these countries. Both Japan and Chile have initiated officially sponsored family planning programs as part of an overall public health effort in controlling abortion. These two countries have totally opposite governmental positions on abortion. Since 1948, when Japan passed the Eugenic

* Note: The authors wish to acknowledge the assistance of Miss Sallie Craig Tuton and Mrs. Emmakate Young in the preparation of this report.

† Chief, Family Planning Evaluation Activity, Epidemiology Program, National Communicable Disease Center, Atlanta, Georgia; Epidemic Intelligence Officer assigned to Department of Gynecology and Obstetrics, Emory University School of Medicine, by Family Planning Evaluation Activity, Epidemiology Program, National Communicable Disease Center, Atlanta, Georgia; and Associate Professor and Chief, Division of Perinatal Pathology, Department of Gynecology and Obstetrics, Emory University School of Medicine, Atlanta, Georgia.

Protection Law, legal abortion has been widely available to the entire population. In Chile, a predominantly Catholic country, abortion is illegal.

## ABORTION IN JAPAN

The widespread use of induced abortion in Japan as a method of fertility control is documented by health statistics and survey data. Furthermore, the demographic changes associated with legalization of abortion in Japan have been profound. Between 1949, the year after passage of the new legislation, and 1959, the number of legal abortions increased from 246,104 to 1,098,853.[1] From 1952 to 1959, "maternal health" as an indication for abortion was reported by physicians in 98.6–99.7 percent of all cases.[2] However, a field survey of women aborted, investigating the true nature of "maternal health" reasons, showed that only 17 percent of the abortions were, in fact, performed for these reasons.[3] Of the remaining 83 percent, 17 percent were performed for child spacing, 50 percent for economic reasons, 13 percent for family size limitation, and 3 percent for unknown reasons.[4]

The crude birth rate in Japan was 33.0 in 1949 and had fallen to 17.5 by 1959.[5] This marked decrease in the birth rate, coinciding with the sharp rise in numbers of legal abortions, provides support for the hypothesis that abortion may have profound demographic significance for an entire nation. However, this is an intricate issue involving a number of variables. As Potts has pointed out, "The impact of legal abortion on the birth rate is difficult to estimate because it involves computing the number of illegal abortions taking place before the law was changed, guessing what might have happened to the criminal abortion rate if the law had not been altered and making an allowance for the changing incidence of contraceptive practices."[6]

The evidence from Japan is clear; induced abortion has been a major means of legal fertility control since 1948.[7] Beyond that, the implication is that the introduction or withdrawal of legal abortion in certain circumstances can result in profound and rapid fertility effects with important demographic consequences.

## ABORTION IN CHILE

In Chile, the first awareness that induced abortion constituted a major public health problem came when it was observed that hospital admissions for incomplete and complicated abortions rose from 12,963 in 1937 to 57,368 in 1960. In spite of a rising percentage of deliveries in hospitals, the ratio of abortions per 1,000 births in hospitals in this twenty-four-year interval nearly tripled, increasing from 84 to 223. Hospital data also revealed 312 deaths due to abortion in 1963, or 38.8 percent of all maternal mortality.[8]

Chilean workers in field surveys in three metropolitan areas —Santiago, Concepción, and Antofagasta—interviewed 3,776 women, 885 of whom, or 23 percent, reported a total of 2,415 induced abortions. In Santiago, nearly one-third (31.5 percent) of these women required hospitalization for the treatment of complications.[9] Results of these surveys confirmed that illegally induced abortion was indeed a major public health problem. The use of abortion as a method of fertility control was substantiated: "With regard to causes for abortion, the importance of (economic reasons) was stressed by nearly 50 percent of the women. Health, large family, conjugal problems, and illegitimacy were outstanding among the remaining causes. However, further analysis showed that ignorance of birth control methods might be considered a basic explanation. Only 29 percent of the women admitted the use of some kind of contraception in Santiago."[10]

## ABORTION CONTROL PROGRAMS IN JAPAN AND CHILE

The earliest attempt at abortion control in Japan was made by the government. In 1950, faced with an increase of 98.7

percent in the number of legal abortions performed, compared with the previous year,[11] the cabinet issued the following statement in November 1951: "Abortion has undesirable
effects on maternal health. It is, therefore, necessary to disseminate contraceptive information to decrease these undesirable effects."[12] As a result, a nationwide plan to promote
conception control was launched in 1952. Judged by the
stated aim of the program, it was a failure. Induced abortions
continued to increase until 1955 when a peak of 1,170,143
was reported. The official evaluation included a number of
reasons explaining the program's lack of success. Among
them were: (1) an inadequate budget, (2) unpaid field
workers, (3) failure of some couples to distinguish between
induced abortion and conception control, and (4) poor cooperation from the obstetrician-gynecologists.[13]

A far more limited but perhaps more realistic attempt at
reducing abortion, by providing contraception, took place
in a relatively circumscribed population of approximately
15,000 persons living in three villages and three coal mining
districts in Japan. A five-year birth control "guidance" program resulted in marked decreases not only in birth rates
per 1,000 population (27.4 to 10.0) but also in the induced
abortion rate per 100 married women (6.3 to 2.1). The conclusion reached was that "a decrease in induced abortion
therefore rests on widespread education among the people
in the effective use of contraception."[14]

A well-documented abortion control program in the western area of Santiago, Chile, was recently described by Viel.[15]
This area has a population of 440,000 persons, including
110,000 women of fertile age. Eighteen percent of the women
of reproductive age were provided contraception, primarily
by inserting intrauterine devices, either immediately following curettage or in the second or third day post partum or
post abortum. This program was carried out over a thirty-
nine-month period. The author summarizes his findings as
follows: "Effects on the community are noted in a reduction

in the number of abortions, calculated to be about 50 percent of the expected, and in a reduction of the birth rate to only 73 percent of that observed the year before the program was begun."[16]

Other Chilean investigators have also reported a decrease both in abortions and births, once contraception was made available on a large scale. In the San Gregorio section of Santiago, a low socioeconomic area with a relatively stable population of 35,000, 30.6 percent of the women, 20 to 34 years of age, were provided contraception, predominantly intrauterine devices. In one year after the program began, the abortion rate declined 31.1 percent and the birth rate was down 26.5 percent.[17]

The most rigorous attempt to evaluate epidemiologically the effect of a birth control program on the prevention of induced abortion is the resurvey in 1967 of the capital city of Santiago, Chile.[18] This work, carried out by the same investigators who conducted the first survey in Santiago in 1962,[19] sought to evaluate the effect of the National Health Service's efforts to provide birth control and prevent abortion in the city. By the end of 1967, it was estimated that the total number of women protected by the program, as well as by private efforts, was 107,047 or 13.0 percent of the women of fertile age in Santiago.[20]

The complexity of evaluating a large-scale program designed to reach all social classes is related to Requeña's hypothesis concerning the interrelationship between socioeconomic level and type of fertility control chosen. "The interrelation between the type of birth control methods of which a community may make use and the social, economic, and cultural level reached is clearly stated in the influence the latter factor has over the former one. Each socioeconomic cultural level will show preference for one of the birth control methods, preferring not to use (any method), if they are a low level; making use of abortion if they are in an intermediate level; and using contraceptives if they are in a high level. According to the way a community changes the proportion of these groups, it will also change the predominance of one of the methods chosen for birth control."[21]

A comparison of the fertility and induced abortion rates in the two one-year periods before the surveys, 1961 and 1966, supported Requeña's hypothesis by showing class-specific changes in abortion rates. Overall fertility declined from 198.7 to 171.2 per 1,000 women, while the induced abortion rate rose from 44.9 to 56.5 per 1,000 women. In the upper and upper-middle socioeconomic level, the abortion rate fell significantly from 36.9 to 24.8. But, in the lower-lower socioeconomic level, the abortion rate increased from 48.8 to 75.3.[22] These findings corroborated Requeña's hypothesis of a transitional stage once a population is motivated to control fertility. Before modern contraceptive methods become widely available, the lowest socioeconomic class of the population turns to abortion as the only recourse, thus, explaining the increase in the abortion rate. The upper class, in contrast, also affected by the educational efforts of the National Health Service, has easier access to contraception and responds with a decrease in its abortion rate.

These results clearly indicate the difficulty in early evaluation of large-scale abortion control programs. In relatively closed populations, however, such as those described above, it is apparent that once contraceptive services are utilized, both fertility and induced abortion decline. Thus, the conclusion: For many individuals, induced abortion is a common method of birth control, and its resultant mortality and morbidity can be reduced by the easy accessibility of more conventional methods.

## ABORTION SURVEILLANCE PROGRAM

The prevention of mortality and morbidity caused by induced abortion requires that the population at risk be described in detail, that a program be initiated to prevent abortion from occurring in this population and that continuous evaluation of the program be established. In an effort to study abortion and its prevention, the Family Planning Evaluation Activity, Epidemiology Program, National Communicable Disease Center, has developed a hospital abortion surveillance project in collaboration with the Department of Gynecology and Obstetrics of the Emory University School of Medicine. This work is supported by the Center for Population Research of the National Institute of Child Health and Human Development. The project is conducted at Grady Memorial Hospital in Atlanta, Georgia. Data collection began in November 1968. This portion of the paper is a preliminary report of the project's first year of activity.

Grady Memorial Hospital is a 1,000-bed municipal hospital which provides inpatient and outpatient care to medically dependent citizens of Fulton and DeKalb Counties, Georgia. Approximately 6,000 obstetrical deliveries occur at the hospital annually. The Emory University Department of Gynecology and Obstetrics supervises obstetrical care at the hospital and provides special services through its Division of Maternal Health and Family Planning, its Maternity and Infant Care Project, and the Division of Perinatal Pathology. The Perinatal Pathology Division assumes direct responsibility for the supervision of this project.

Under this surveillance system, all women who come to the hospital with complications of abortion are asked by a member of the hospital staff if they have had an induced abortion. All those who acknowledge that they have undergone such a procedure are admitted to the hospital, as are all other women with significant complications, principally hemorrhage and infection, which may result from spontaneous as well as from induced abortions. The treatment for each patient is determined by her physical findings.

The project staff then interviews all women hospitalized with a diagnosis of abortion. These interviews have no effect on the subsequent medical care provided. Those who acknowledge that they have had an induced abortion on the preliminary interview are so diagnosed, and given an inter-

view in depth. The remaining patients are assumed to have
had a spontaneous miscarriage and they receive a detailed interview in selected cases only. All respondents are questioned
about their contraceptive use prior to the pregnancy just
terminated, and they receive a post-abortion referral to the
Emory University Family Planning Program clinic, located
in the same hospital.

In the first six months of the project, 374 abortions were
reported. During the same time, there were 2,909 live births,
giving a ratio of 128.6 abortions per 1,000 live births. Although most of these abortions occurred in Negro women,
the ratio of abortions to live births at Grady Hospital was
greater for whites than for Negroes. The ratio for women
of all ethnic groups increased with maternal age. Thirty-seven
abortions, of which 10 were in-hospital, were induced, while
337 were reported as spontaneous. Fever was more common
among women who admitted having an induced abortion.
Nearly half the patients with induced abortion (44.4 percent)
had an oral temperature of 100.4° Fahrenheit or greater at
the time of admission to the hospital, whereas only 12.8 percent of patients with spontaneous abortion had similar temperature elevations when first seen. Of the 27 women who
came to the hospital with complications of nontherapeutic
induced abortion, 22 stated that they were not married, while
approximately half of those with spontaneous abortions were
unmarried. Of the women treated for nontherapeutic induced
abortion during this six-month period, 12 of 13 whites, or 92.3
percent, had come to Grady Hospital for the first time, while
none of the 14 Negro women were new to the hospital.

Of the 10 therapeutic abortions authorized and performed
during this six-month period, 7 involved white women and 3
were for Negro women, corresponding to ratios of 13.1 and
1.3 per 1,000 live births, respectively. Five of the 7 white
patients were new to Grady Hospital, while none of the 3
Negro women were in this category.

Women who have had induced nontherapeutic abortions

TABLE 1.

NUMBER AND PERCENT DISTRIBUTION OF PATIENTS WITH
INDUCED ABORTION, BY TYPE OF INDUCTION AND DEM-
OGRAPHIC CHARACTERISTICS: GRADY MEMORIAL HOSPI-
TAL, ATLANTA, GEORGIA, NOVEMBER 1968–
OCTOBER 1969.

| Characteristic | Therapeutic abortion | | Nontherapeutic abortion | | Total | |
|---|---|---|---|---|---|---|
| | Number | Percent | Number | Percent | Number | Percent |
| Total | 30 | 100.0 | 60 | 100.0 | 90 | 100.0 |
| Ethnic group: | | | | | | |
| White | 17 | 56.7 | 31 | 51.7 | 48 | 53.3 |
| Negro | 13 | 43.3 | 29 | 48.3 | 42 | 46.7 |
| Age: | | | | | | |
| Less than 15 | 5 | 16.7 | 1 | 1.7 | 6 | 6.7 |
| 15–19 | 4 | 13.3 | 14 | 23.3 | 18 | 20.0 |
| 20–24 | 11 | 36.7 | 31 | 51.7 | 42 | 46.7 |
| 25–29 | 4 | 13.3 | 11 | 18.3 | 15 | 16.7 |
| 30–34 | 5 | 16.7 | 2 | 3.3 | 7 | 7.8 |
| 35 or more | 1 | 3.3 | 1 | 1.7 | 2 | 2.2 |
| Marital status: | | | | | | |
| Married | 4 | 13.3 | 9 | 15.0 | 13 | 14.4 |
| Single | 17 | 56.7 | 37 | 61.7 | 54 | 60.0 |
| Separated, widowed, or divorced | 9 | 30.0 | 14 | 23.3 | 23 | 25.6 |

are more likely to suffer medical complications than those whose abortions occurred spontaneously. For this preliminary report on the first full year of the program, therefore, priority has been given to the analysis of data on the 90 women treated at Grady Hospital with a diagnosis of induced abortion. Data on all those with a diagnosis of spontaneous abortion during this twelve-month period will be presented in a future report. Demographic characteristics of the 90 women with induced abortion, tabulated by type of induction, are presented in Table 1. Forty-eight of the 90 women or 53.3 percent were white, and 42 women or 46.7 percent were Negro. There is no significant difference in the racial distribution by type of induced abortion. However, of the women delivering live-born infants at Grady Hospital in the first half of this year, 81.6 percent were Negro and 18.4 percent were white. All but 15 of the 90 women were between 15 and 30 years old, 6 or 6.7 percent were younger than 15 years, and 9 women or 10 percent, were 30 years or older. The median age of the group was 22.7 years. The distribution by marital status shows that the 54 women who had never been married make up 60.0 percent of the total group, while 13 or 14.4 percent were married at the time of their abortion. The remaining 23

## TABLE 2.

### NUMBER AND PERCENT DISTRIBUTION OF PATIENTS WITH IN-DUCED ABORTION, BY TYPE OF INDUCTION, WEEKS OF GESTATION, AND CONTRACEPTIVE HISTORY: GRADY MEMORIAL HOSPITAL, ATLANTA, GEORGIA, NOVEMBER 1968–OCTOBER 1969.

| Gestation and contraceptive history | Therapeutic abortion | | Nontherapeutic abortion | | Total | |
|---|---|---|---|---|---|---|
| | Number | Percent | Number | Percent | Number | Percent |
| Weeks of gestation: | | | | | | |
| 0–4 | .. | .... | 1 | 1.7 | 1 | 1.1 |
| 5–9 | .. | .... | 11 | 18.3 | 11 | 12.2 |
| 10–14 | 13 | 43.3 | 31 | 51.7 | 44 | 48.9 |
| 15–19 | 13 | 43.3 | 12 | 20.0 | 25 | 27.8 |
| 20 or more | 4 | 13.3 | 5 | 8.3 | 9 | 10.0 |
| Contraceptive clinic attendance: | | | | | | |
| *Pre-operative* | | | | | | |
| Yes | 8 | 26.7 | 12 | 20.0 | 20 | 22.2 |
| No | 22 | 73.3 | 48 | 80.0 | 70 | 77.8 |
| *Postoperative*[1] | | | | | | |
| Accepted | 26 | 86.7 | 41 | 69.5 | 67 | 75.3 |
| Not accepted | 4 | 13.3 | 18 | 30.5 | 22 | 24.7 |

[1] Excludes one patient who died shortly after admission.

women or 25.6 percent were separated, widowed, or divorced.

Table 2 shows the number of weeks of pregnancy which had elapsed by the time these women underwent induced abortion, and their pre- and postoperative contraceptive history. All but 9 of the women had their abortions between the tenth and the nineteenth week of pregnancy. The median weeks of gestation for women having therapeutic abortions, however, was 15.8, compared with 12.9 weeks for those who had a nontherapeutic abortion. Twenty or 22.2 percent of the women had previously attended the Emory University Family Planning Program clinic, as documented in the clinic's records.

The prevention of repeatedly induced abortion in the patients under study requires the prevention of future unwanted pregnancies because their willingness to use abortion as a method of fertility control is already proven. Of the 90 women, 67 or 75.3 percent accepted contraception after their treatment at the hospital for the complications of this procedure. This is comparable to unpublished data showing that 76.8 percent of women delivering either full-term or premature births at Grady Hospital in 1968 accepted postpartum contraception. The data show, however, that the women with a diagnosis of nontherapeutic abortion accepted contraception less often than those who had a therapeutic abortion done in the hospital.

Table 3 distributes the women admitted with a diagnosis of nontherapeutic abortion by ethnic group, and shows that the acceptance of contraception following abortion is substantially less for white women than for Negro women with this diagnosis.

These data indicate that there are problems requiring further investigation. The white women in this study are obviously different from the majority of women who come to Grady Hospital as maternity patients. A greater proportion of white women come to this hospital with abortion problems than come to deliver live infants. These women with com-

## TABLE 3.

NONTHERAPEUTIC INDUCED ABORTION PATIENTS BY
ACCEPTANCE OF POSTOPERATIVE CONTRACEPTION AND
ETHNIC GROUP TREATED AT GRADY MEMORIAL
HOSPITAL, ATLANTA, GEORGIA.

| Postoperative contraception | Ethnic group | | | | Total | |
|---|---|---|---|---|---|---|
| | White | | Negro | | | |
| | Number | Percent | Number | Percent | Number | Percent |
| Total | 31 | 100.0 | 28 | 100.0 | 59[1] | 100.0 |
| Accepted | 16 | 51.6 | 25 | 89.3 | 41 | 69.5 |
| Not accepted | 15 | 48.4 | 3 | 10.7 | 18 | 30.5 |

1 One patient who died shortly after admission to the hospital is excluded.

plications of abortion are often seeking care at this hospital
for the first time. After receiving treatment, they are less likely
to accept contraception than their Negro counterparts. They
live in upper and middle class sections of the city or in well-
to-do suburbs. These facts suggest that white women coming
to the municipal hospital with complications of abortion have
a discontinuity of health care. Having initially been rejected
by, or having chosen to reject, their usual sources of medical
care they sought other medical aid for their abortion problem.
Then, having solved that problem, nearly half of the women
refused further care aimed at preventing its recurrence.

Another point, mentioned briefly in connection with Table
2, raises a second issue for discussion. Therapeutic abortions
were performed later in pregnancy, on the average, than were
nontherapeutic abortions (Table 2). Since data on induced
abortions from other parts of the world suggest that the
mortality and morbidity associated with the abortion procedure increases with gestational age, such a finding has important implications for the safety of therapeutic abortion
patients. A number of possibilities might offer an explanation
of this finding, assuming that the difference between these
groups persists as the series is enlarged. The women who had
therapeutic abortions may not have been aware that they were

pregnant as soon as those who had nontherapeutic abortions. Another possibility is that personal ambivalence may have led those receiving therapeutic abortions to hesitate in making their requests for this operation. It is possible, too, that the process by which therapeutic abortions are authorized and performed requires analysis. Data from the first six months of this project support our concern on this issue. Therapeutic abortion patients spent 12.7 days in the hospital, on the average, while women with a diagnosis of nontherapeutic abortion were hospitalized for an average of only 6.2 days. Of the 442 days spent in the hospital by therapeutic abortion patients, 277 or 62.7 percent were preoperative. This time was used primarily for evaluation of each case. The numbers in these groups are small, but they point to a problem in the management of hospital abortion cases which is important.

## SUMMARY

In summarizing these preliminary findings from the abortion surveillance project at Grady Hospital, the following points deserve emphasis:

1. This project has provided epidemiologic data which are basic to the study and prevention of abortion mortality and morbidity. Analysis of these data suggests an approach to the problem which is worth attempting in other settings.

2. In the first six months of this project, 374 patients with a diagnosis of abortion were treated at Grady Hospital. Ten of them had therapeutic abortions.

3. Preliminary analyses of women with induced abortions indicate that nontherapeutic induced abortion patients at this hospital differ from other obstetrical patients. They are more often white. Frequently coming to the hospital for the first time, they appear to lack continuity in their maternal health care. Of the 31 white patients, 15 refused postabortion contraception offered to prevent future unwanted pregnancies.

## RESEARCH NEEDS AND METHODS

Two issues pertinent to the abortion problem deserve priority consideration for research. First, because abortion is a major and persistent cause of maternal mortality, more accurate information on the extent to which abortion complications cause death is needed.[23] Although reports on mortality have been a part of national data collection since 1902, the accuracy with which abortion deaths are reported is open to question. In 1966, twenty of fifty states which account for more than half a million births in this country reported no deaths due to abortion.[24] While this is possible, it seems most unlikely. Personal experience has shown that individual cases of deaths due to abortion have been reported as fever of unknown origin or as enterocolitis without mention of the fact that the decedents were recently pregnant. If mortality and morbidity due to abortion are to be controlled in this country, then their accurate measure is essential in order to define the magnitude of the problem and to evaluate the effects of the public health efforts taken to solve it.

The second major issue requiring research is the extent to which abortion is used as a method of birth control. The experience of other countries shows that in some parts of the world abortion is the principal means by which women control their family size. In our own country, however, there is a striking lack of information on this subject. The importance of the relationship between abortion and contraception is emphasized by the programs of other nations in which a decline in the abortion rate has been associated with an increase in the provision of contraceptive services. More knowledge about this relationship will be needed if the problems associated with induced abortion are to be prevented in our own country.

Having identified the issues in need of research, the next task is to suggest methods for conducting investigations on these subjects. The development of an intensified surveillance system of maternal deaths is a logical first step in measuring the level of mortality attributable to abortion. Such a system should provide for systematic collection of pertinent data, orderly and regular consolidation and evaluation of these data, and the prompt dissemination of the results to all people who need to know this information. This kind of surveillance should be nationwide and logically fits into existing mortality reporting responsibilities of public health agencies.

Routine reporting activities will need to be supplemented by special studies. In order to estimate the extent to which abortion deaths are underreported, intensive study, including pathological examination of all women who die between the ages of 15 and 49, should be carried out in localities where such studies can be implemented. Additional field studies, regarded as an integral part of surveillance in communicable disease control, should also be a part of this system. Specific cases, or even clusters of cases, are likely to require on the spot investigation by those responsible for interpreting surveillance data.

Therapeutic abortion surveillance on a national basis is a logical and important part of abortion research. These data will make available important information to those concerned with health services and legislative change, as well as those interested in maternal health and family well-being.

Surveillance of hospital admissions of women with a diagnosis of abortion will be needed from selected localities. The abortion surveillance project at Grady Hospital is an example of this kind of research. Information from a hospital-based surveillance system will be useful in monitoring abortion morbidity and gaining information needed to improve medical management of complications of induced abortions and therapeutic abortions.

Operational studies of hospital abortion authorization and performance will be essential to the public interest. Recent legal changes have resulted in an increased demand for abortions in hospitals. If hospital stay and length of disability are to be minimized, then it will be necessary to study the ways in which a woman is evaluated prior to her abortion, the way she responds to the abortion, or its refusal. Hospital data will also permit an evaluation of the different operative techniques used in performing therapeutic abortion.

In measuring the extent to which abortion is used as a method of birth control, survey research will be essential. Such surveys will permit estimates of the total number of women who undergo abortion and whether they seek hospital care. This is important information which a surveillance system cannot provide. A nationwide sample survey is a logical step in this area when valid interview techniques are available. Subsequently, or perhaps concurrently, regional and community surveys should be performed to provide data on specific problems. As this information is gathered, it, like surveillance data, should be made immediately available to all those who have a need to know.

## RECOMMENDATIONS

In order to gain support for a research program appropriate to the magnitude of the abortion problem, a national policy decision to eliminate maternal death due to abortion is needed. Such a policy would be both acceptable and timely. The speed with which legal change governing the practice of abortion is taking place in most regions of the nation suggests that national action in the area of abortion and health would receive wide approval. The commitment of the Federal Government to make contraceptive service available to those in need is one of the key features in a program aimed at preventing abortion mortality. The fact that the President took note of illegal abortion as a health problem in his population message is a further indication that our country is ready to make abortion a subject of national policy.[25]

A corollary to this is that research priorities should be determined by the degree to which specific investigations contribute to such a program. The prevention of maternal deaths due to abortion should be the stated goal of national policy and the guiding concept in a program of support for abortion research.

## NOTES

1. Muramatsu, M., *Japan's Experience in Family Planning—Past and Present* (Tokyo: Family Planning Federation of Japan, Inc., 1967), Table 29, p. 69.

2. *Ibid.*, Table 34, p. 73.

3. Koya, Y.; Muramatsu, M.; Agata, S.; and Koya, T., "Preliminary report of a survey of health and demographic aspects of induced abortion in Japan," *Archives of the Population Association of Japan*, 2:1–9 (1953).

4. *Ibid.*

5. Muramatsu, M., *Japan's Experience in Family Planning*, Table 3, p. 16.

6. Potts, M., "Legal abortion in Eastern Europe," *Eugenics Review*, 59:232–250 (December 1967).

7. Tietze, C., and Lewit, S., "Abortion," *Scientific American*, 220:21–27 (January 1969).

8. Armijo, R., and Monreal, T., "The problem of induced abortion in Chile," *Milbank Memorial Fund Quarterly*, 43:263–280 (October 1965).

9. Armijo, R., and Monreal, T., "Factors associated with complications following provoked abortion," *Journal of Sex Research*, 4:1–6, (February 1963).

10. Armijo and Monreal, "Induced abortion," p. 270.

11. Muramatsu, M., *Japan's Experience in Family Planning*, Table 29, p. 69.

12. *Ibid.*, p. 87.

13. *Ibid.*, p. 93.

14. Koya, Y., "Why induced abortions in Japan remain high," *Research in Family Planning* (ed. C. V. Kiser) (Princeton: Princeton University Press, 1962), pp. 103–110.

15. Viel, B., "Results of a family planning program in the Western Area of the city of Santiago," *American Journal of Public Health*, 59:1898–1909 (October 1969).

16. *Ibid.*

17. Requeña, M., and Monreal, T., "Evaluation of induced abortion

control and family planning programs in Chile," *Milbank Memorial Fund Quarterly*, 46:191–218 (July 1968).

18. Monreal, T., and Armijo, R., "Evaluacion del programa de prevencion del aborto provocado en Santiago," *Revista Medica de Chile*, 96:605–622 (September 1963).

19. Armijo, R., and Monreal, T., "Epidemiology of provoked abortions in Santiago, Chile," *Journal of Sex Research*, 1:143–159 (July 1965).

20. Monreal and Armijo, "prevencion delaborto provocado."

21. Requeña, M., Program of comparative studies of induced abortion and usage of contraceptives in Latin America, provisional edition (January 1967).

22. Monreal and Armijo, "prevencion delaborto provocado."

23. National Center for Health Statistics, *Infant, Fetal, and Maternal Mortality: United States—1963*, Series 20, Number 3, pp. 54–61.

24. National Center for Health Statistics, *Vital Statistics of the United States, Vol. II, Mortality, Part B* (Washington, D.C.: U. S. Government Printing Office, 1966).

25. Nixon, R. M., "Problems of Population Growth," The President's Message to the Congress, Including His Proposal for the Creation of a Commission on Population Growth and the American Future (July 13, 1969).

# Induced Abortion and Contraception: Sociological Aspects

Emily C. Moore M.A., M.S.*

ALTHOUGH induced abortion and contraception are often viewed as alternatives, total fertility control includes both pregnancy prevention and pregnancy termination—the "fireproofing" and the "fire extinguisher."

There are several possible life patterns which the individual woman may follow: no contraception, no abortion; regular contraceptive practice, and accidental pregnancies carried to term; regular contraceptive practice, abortion used to terminate accidental pregnancies; initial use of contraception, then a change to reliance on abortion; one or more abortions, then a change to reliance on contraception; continuous reliance on abortion alone; sporadic reliance on either or both methods combined.

The following sections bring together available evidence on the relationship between abortion and contraception.

* Staff Associate, Demographic Division, The Population Council, New York, New York.

## RELATIVE MERITS OF INDUCED ABORTION AND CONTRACEPTION

### MEDICAL ASPECTS

From a medical point of view, which is the preferred means of fertility control? If mortality is the sole criterion for judging a method's medical merits, we may conclude from the model proposed by Tietze that a combination of perfectly safe but not entirely effective contraception and in-hospital abortion to terminate contraceptive failures entails the lowest risk.[1]

### PERSONAL ASPECTS

Why is abortion used so widely, even when contraceptive techniques are known and available; i.e., why is it often preferable from the woman's point of view? Some suggested answers are the following:

1. Except for sterilization and the IUD, no other birth-prevention technique is a one-event procedure. (Injections and implants are once-every-three-to-four-months, possibly once-a-year actions.)

2. Abortion does not require the knowledge or consent of the husband.

3. It is coitus-independent, as are IUD's and orals.

4. Unlike nearly all contraceptives (except for injections, implants, and continuous conscientious use of the pill), once begun it is 100 percent effective, although attempts may be unsuccessful. Perhaps it should be stated instead that there is continuous uncertainty associated with the use of most contraceptives, whereas the woman knows almost immediately whether or not an abortion attempt has been successful. Unsuccessful abortion attempts are certainly difficult to enumerate and have a wide range in terms of seriousness of intent and degree of effort.

5. Abortion is not based on the probabilities of conception,

but on the certainty of a recognized pregnancy; i.e., it requires hindsight, not foresight; is curative, not preventive. The small proportion of coital acts which result in pregnancy may encourage many women to "take a chance" and be unprotected.

6. Abortion is the only method to avert a birth which may have been desired at the time of conception but which, due to changed circumstances, may no longer be wanted.

7. Compared with mechanical and chemical means, abortion is technically simple. For the unmarried, separated, widowed, or divorced, with infrequent or unanticipated intercourse, abortion is possibly cheaper and/or more appropriate than other methods.

ECONOMIC ASPECTS

Three considerations must be included here: cost to the woman and to society of (1) abortion, (2) various means of contraception, and (3) combinations of the two.

Where abortion is either illicitly performed or legally obtained only with great difficulty and expense, contraception is less costly to the woman. Where abortion is provided by the state free or with minimal cost, and there is a charge for contraceptive services, the reverse is true. Where both are free, the woman will not be influenced in her choice by cost factors.

Abortions legally performed are usually said to be more costly to society than the provision of contraceptive services or the provision of neither; however, providing contraceptive services alone or neither contraception nor abortion may result in the necessity for hospital emergency care of illegally induced abortions. The comparative costs to society of hospital bed-days, transfusions, antibiotics, laboratory use, and time of medical and paramedical personnel, for abortion only, for contraception only, or for both or neither have not been determined.

The medical profession's willingness or reluctance to provide contraceptive services or to perform abortions or deliveries, and the payment they receive for each of these tasks may be important determinants of relative use. There appear, however, to have been few attempts to document this.

## RELATIONSHIP BETWEEN ABORTION AND CONTRACEPTION—MUTUAL EFFECTS

### ATTITUDES

Westoff, Moore, and Ryder found a direct relationship between positive attitudes toward contraception and more liberal views on abortion; the relationship held true regardless of race or religion.[2]

Girard and Zucker obtained similar results in France; opposition to abortion was positively related to opposition to contraception.[3]

### KNOWLEDGE

While a number of attitude surveys on the subject of abortion have been conducted in the United States, Japan, Great Britain, and elsewhere, almost no attempt has been made to determine the level of knowledge about abortion. Thus, it is not yet possible to compare abortion knowledge with contraceptive knowledge in the same community, nor to see how attitudes vary with level of knowledge.

In a pilot survey conducted in Washington Heights, New York City, in 1968–1969 in response to the question "Would you please tell me how abortions are done," 38 percent of 169 women expressed no knowledge whatsoever of any medically acceptable method of inducing abortion.[4] Even "see a doctor" was considered knowledge of acceptable method; i.e., 38 percent described only folk methods or no method at all. Among a number of variables with which "some knowledge" was positively associated was the respondent's approval of contraception and knowledge of modern contraceptive methods. She was not asked if she knew how or where to obtain an abortion.

## EITHER/OR

It is sometimes suggested for the individual seeking abortion that "she should have used contraceptives," when she is clearly already pregnant. It has been proposed that sterilization should follow every legal abortion, or that a mass sterilization program would obviate the need for abortions. These proposals ignore the variety of circumstances, such as rape, rubella, an unmarried woman, an unstable marriage, or a woman suffering from a temporary illness in which a particular pregnancy may be unwanted but a future one welcomed.

A clear distinction needs to be made between the individual family's requirements for satisfactory fertility control and society's requirements: a society may decide that funds are better invested in contraceptive programs rather than in legal abortions, or vice versa, although concentration on one to the exclusion of the other may be unsatisfactory to individuals and their families who might prefer to have access to both.

## AVAILABILITY AND MOTIVATION

To what extent either abortion or contraception is used may be determined less by individual preference than by availability. Access to abortion and contraception may vary widely according to region, income, local climate of opinion, age, range of permissible indications, and even the time at which a request is submitted relative to the filling of monthly quotas; thus, the "choice" between abortion, contraception, and delivery may not be based at all on reasons noted.

Romania and immediately postwar Japan are especially conspicuous for high rates of abortion and nonavailability of modern contraceptives.[5] High rates of legal abortion among the unmarried in Great Britain may be partially due to their difficulty in obtaining contraception.[6] Nonavailability is a determining factor varying not only by marital status but by region as well: of 200 local health authorities, only 34 provide "full family planning service."[7]

Sometimes access to both abortion and contraception is limited: U.S. hospitals with the most restrictive abortion policies tend also to provide the least contraceptive services.[8] The consequences are higher rates of delivery, illegal abortion, and/or contraceptive services from private physicians or clinics in the areas served by such hospitals.

Hubinont has noted the inverse relationship between active family planning programs and estimated abortion rates in European countries.[9] He concludes that such programs apparently have more effect than the provisions of abortion laws on the frequency of abortion.

It has been suggested that abortion and contraception merely provide the means for fertility control when motivation already exists. "The use of abortion on a mass scale as a means of birth prevention is not the result of government policy; on the contrary, it was public pressure on the government which made legally available, on a very wide basis, a form of control which had been embedded in the social customs of Tokugawa, Japan."[10] However, ease of access may also enhance desire. Some who argue that liberalization of abortion laws would have an insignificant effect in India, for example, note that motivation for small families already existed in Japan and eastern Europe prior to liberalization of abortion laws but does not yet exist in India. Others contend that surveys in India, demonstrating a "desired family size" notably smaller than "actual family size," indicate a reservoir of ready motivation for use of abortion should it become legally available. Motivation for control of family size, while already substantial before liberalization in Japan and eastern Europe, must have been greatly stimulated when abortions became more easily obtainable, since birth rates, already declining, decreased even more sharply thereafter.

USE OF ABORTION; USE OF CONTRACEPTION

Let us now examine the evidence for various contentions regarding the effects of abortion and contraception on each other. The case is sometimes based on small nonrepresentative samples and insufficient evidence, but the accumulation of data and analysis from a variety of situations makes it possible for us to draw some tentative conclusions. Where abortion remains an illicit act, or at least a private matter, data remains sketchy and analysis restricted by necessary estimates and conjectures.

Possible combinations are the following:

Static situations (either unchanging conditions, or a situation which is investigated at only one point in time):

1. Low contraceptive use    High abortion incidence
2. High contraceptive use   Low abortion incidence
3. Low contraceptive use    Low abortion incidence
4. High contraceptive use   High abortion incidence

Dynamic situations (investigated in before-after situations):

5. Liberalization of abortion law raises contraceptive use.
6. Liberalization of abortion law lowers contraceptive use.
7. Restriction of liberal abortion law raises contraceptive use.
8. Restriction of liberal abortion law lowers contraceptive use.
9. Introduction of family planning program raises abortion incidence.
10. Introduction of family planning program lowers abortion incidence, either immediately or after some delay.

A clear distinction should be made between abortion *rates* per population, or per woman, and abortion *ratios* per pregnancies, or per live births. A population using contraception successfully may have a very low abortion rate, but a very high abortion ratio; i.e., there may be a major reliance on contraception, but once an unplanned pregnancy occurs, it is very likely to be aborted.

1. In the absence of availability of contraception, is abortion incidence (rates and ratios) likely to be high, particularly in a culture with a small family norm?

It is not surprising that among eastern European countries, the highest abortion rates and ratios have been recorded in Romania (before the 1967 change in its law) and in Hungary, the two eastern European countries with reportedly very poor use of contraceptives and extremely low birth rates (14.3 in Romania, 1966, and 14.5 in Hungary, 1967). Examples from developing countries could also be cited.

2. Where there has long been access to and widespread use of contraception, is abortion incidence correspondingly lower? That is, can low abortion rates (per population) be expected, even if abortion ratios (per pregnancies or live births) are high?

According to Hubinont, "The existence of family planning services and the absence of legal restrictions on the access to contraception [in western Europe] does indeed correspond with a lower estimate of the incidence of illegal abortion."[11]

The United States is considered a highly "contracepting" population with a relatively low estimated abortion rate. Declaring abortion rates either "high" or "low" in countries where only a small proportion are legally performed, is however, a precarious undertaking.

3. Illustrating low contraceptive use and low abortion rates and ratios are societies with unusually high fertility; e.g., Hutterites in the United States.

4. High contraceptive use coupled with high abortion ratios can best be illustrated by the studies which find that individuals who abort tend also to contracept, and vice versa, more than their counterparts in the same society.

   a. Are aborters more likely to be contraceptors than are nonaborters? Evidence from Israel, Brazil, Taiwan, Japan, South Korea suggest this is so.[12] The last example, the Seoul survey, reports that while current users of contraceptives constituted only 9 percent of the total sample, 48 percent of the women who had aborted were practicing contraception.

b. Are contraceptors more likely to resort to abortion than noncontraceptors? Evidence from studies in Taiwan, India, Greece, Chile, and Japan supports this contention.[13]

Women who use contraceptives, of course, are selected strongly for a higher motivation toward fertility control. They are likely to resort to abortion when their contraceptive efforts fail. The greater the expectation of avoiding pregnancy, the greater is the likelihood of an induced abortion once a pregnancy has occurred.

5. Liberalization of abortion laws raises contraceptive use.

This is an unlikely occurrence in the absence of a deliberate effort to cause it to occur, although increased use of both methods of fertility control may logically occur simultaneously. Most proponents of liberalized abortion laws stress the desirability of extending contraceptive use and discouraging use of abortion wherever possible.

On an individual level, an unpleasant experience with abortion may inspire a woman to begin or improve contraceptive use.

6. Liberalization of abortion laws lowers contraceptive use.

It is sometimes suggested that the consequence of liberalization of abortion laws in eastern Europe has been to weaken reliance on contraception. However, the evidence is scanty,* and there is contrary evidence to suggest that concerted efforts to encourage contraceptive use can prevent such undesirable

---

* Szabady and Klinger state that ten years after liberalization, roughly the same proportions are using some method of contraception, but there was an apparent shift to less reliable methods, which may, however, have been due to the survey method. The same may not occur in a population using better methods to begin with. Szabady, E., and Klinger, A., "The 1965-66 Hungarian study on fertility, family planning, and birth control," *Demográfia*, 9:135–161, 1966.

effects. Moreover, the contraceptives in use were primarily
traditional methods; evidence from societies in which more
modern methods are in widespread use and in which abortion
laws are then liberalized (Great Britain, and some states of
the United States) has not yet been obtained.

7. Restriction of legal abortion laws raises contraceptive
use.

Romania and Bulgaria are the only recent examples of a
situation in which a permissive abortion law has become less
so. Bulgaria's change was not so drastic, and data on contraceptive use are lacking. Following an initial rise in birth rates
after de-liberalization in Romania, apparent control over
fertility in that country indicates some increased reliance on
contraception as well as on illegal abortion.

8. Restriction of liberal abortion laws lowers contraceptive
use.

This is unlikely and unknown to date. It is conceivable
that lowered contraceptive use and more restrictive abortion
laws might simultaneously occur in a situation of strongly
coercive pronatalist policy—restriction of abortion law plus
restriction on importation, manufacture, and distribution of
contraceptives.

9. Introduction of a family planning program raises abortion incidence.

There is evidence from Korea, Taiwan, and Chile to suggest
this unanticipated and undesirable event.[14]

The discovery that abortions may increase after the introduction of measures designed to cause abortions to decrease
must be a disappointment to program administrators. There
are indications, however, that this may be a transitional state
of affairs. "A Family Planning program carries with it an
awakening to the necessity for limiting the family in many
marginal sectors, beyond the possibilities of local services, and
this, added to the failures of contraceptives in use, will lead
to the interruption of pregnancies already undesired."[15]

10. Have we any evidence that a family planning pro-

gram can lower abortion incidence either immediately or eventually?

a. Reduced abortion *without* an intervening period of increased abortion seems to have been the case in Denmark, where a decline in abortions started at the same time as the "enlightenment" campaign of the Danish Family Planning Association;[16] in Poland, Czechoslovakia, and Yugoslavia, where the adoption of active family planning policies in recent years has been accompanied by a plateau or slight dropping off in abortions;[17] and in Yugoslavia, where an experiment was conducted in Belgrade, Subotica, and Sarajevo, utilizing randomly selected alternate postabortal patients for experimental and control groups.[18] The control group had the same access to family planning as the general population, while the experimental group was given intensive exposure to family planning education. After three years, the results were that 99.2 percent of the experimental and 37.7 percent of the control group were using contraception; the former had significantly lower repeat abortion experience; 124 legal abortions were performed during the study period on experimental women and 508 on control women.

Faundes reports that abortion rates in Chile have fallen significantly between 1964 (before the institution of an intensive family planning education-and-services project in 1965) and 1968.[19]

Accounting for the differences between the findings in San Gregorio and those of Monreal and Armijo, Faundes, et al. suggest:[20]

> There are some differences between both programs that may explain why the rates of abortion decreased in San Gregorio and not in the rest of the Southern Area [of Santiago]. One of these differences refers to the capacity of the clinics, that in many sectors of the Southern Area—with the exception of San Gregorio— is insufficient to satisfy the demand for a quick and timely assistance. Delays and rejections are therefore frequent. . . . Another difference is related with the location of the clinics. In the South-

ern Area there are extensive zones with large population that do not have contraceptive services. This implies that many women have to travel relatively long distances for attention, which makes it difficult not only to begin the use of a contraceptive but also to obtain an adequate follow-up and opportune advice or treatment of inter-current conditions.

b. Reduced abortion incidence *with* an intervening period of increased abortion may have occurred in Taiwan, where "the annual incidence of induced abortion among the respondents of the 1967 island-wide KAP survey significantly increased between 1964 and 1965. The increase after 1965 was rather small. The island-wide family planning program was started in January 1964 . . . the program might have caused an increase in the incidence of induced abortion, particularly at the initial stage."[21] Although actual reduction is not yet observed, the rise appears to have slowed down or halted. In Japan, the annual number of live births remains steady and reported abortion rates are steadily declining; either contraceptive practice *is* improving and reducing the need for abortion, or the reporting of abortion is deteriorating.

In 1952, concerned by the rapid rise in induced abortion, the Japanese Minister of Health urged all local areas to increase contraceptive education and services. Several experiments at introducing family planning intensively in villages were initiated, and accumulated evidence indicates that following an initial rise in abortions, the rates of abortions eventually dropped off*—more rapidly than the overall decrease for Japan as a whole.[22]

The small-scale intensive efforts to promote contraceptive success demonstrated in Japan, Chile, and Yugoslavia would be difficult to extend to an entire nation. A changeover from reliance on abortion to contraception does seem to be feasible, but concerted efforts appear to be needed and large-scale illustrations are still lacking.

* *Ratios*—abortions per live births—generally increased, reflecting a stronger motivation to eliminate unwanted births.

We have noted that the presence of a family planning program may initially stimulate the abortion rate; it may do so by motivating acceptors whose contraceptives fail to persist in their initial intention to prevent births, and by motivating persons for whom contraceptive services are not immediately available. Two crucial considerations for those initiating a family planning program would seem to be whether or not widespread services can be set up rapidly enough to service the newly motivated, and whether or not the program should assume responsibility for the increased number of abortions which result from program stimulated motivation which is followed by method failure.

Monreal and Armijo express their view on this matter:[28]

> Leaving cultural prejudices aside, it may be asked if it would be more suitable, at least in those cases of the failure of contraceptives recommended by the health services, to use the same services for induced abortion. Without doubt, this would diminish the risks and acknowledge a necessity strongly felt by Chilean women at this time.
>
> This means that the fight against induced abortion should be carried on with a new mentality which will consider its incorporation in the prevention programs.

And later, quite explicitly, they state:

> It is suggested that induced abortion ought to be considered in the programs of prevention of abortion and family planning and should be carried out by the Health Services especially in those cases where contraceptives have failed.

It should be noted that such a policy is already in practice, in a limited fashion, in the Tunisian family planning program where women with five or more living children are aborted on request as part of the program's activities. The Tunisian law on abortion was changed in order to permit the incorporation of abortion in the family planning program.

Requeña has suggested a diagram (Figure 1) which illustrates the three stages through which a society may pass, from no birth prevention, to primary reliance on abortion, and to major reliance on contraception with some residual abortions to "mop up" when contraceptives fail. The diagram presents stages over time through which a society passes, as well as concurrent patterns observed in three strata of society at one point in time.

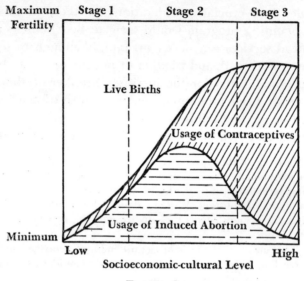

FIGURE 1

If Requeña's diagram accurately illustrates the necessary stages through which a society must pass, it would seem unlikely that the interim (abortion) stage could be easily or quickly bypassed.[24]

## DEMOGRAPHIC EFFECTS OF ABORTION AND/OR CONTRACEPTION

Abortion can clearly be a powerful agent in averting births, even though it must occur with great frequency, when used exclusively. In fact, it is in situations in which abortion has been the primary factor (such as Japan and Romania) that the most dramatic changes in births over short periods of time have been observed.

Used in combination with contraception, it can theoretically be even more effective, as shown by Potter, i.e., it need be resorted to less frequently in order to have important impact.[25] Potter reasons that in a noncontracepting population, the average time involved in induced abortion is 9 months, including 5 months of ovulatory exposure; for a live birth it is 21 months (30 months if lactation is prolonged). Under these conditions, 100 induced abortions account for 900 months of marriage duration, during which 43 (900/21 months) or 30 (900/30 months) live births might have occurred. Thus 100 abortions are needed to avert 43 or 30 live births (roughly 2 or 3 to 1).

When combined with effective contraception, an induced abortion becomes more nearly equivalent to averting a live birth. Assuming 90 percent effectiveness of contraception, the mean length of ovulatory exposure is increased from 5 months to 50 months. One hundred induced abortions now require 5,400 months of marriage duration, equivalent to 81.8 live births with no lactation (5,400/66 months) and 72 births if lactation is prolonged (5,400/75 months).

Only rarely is an attempt made to attribute proportionate amounts of total fertility decline in real populations to abortion and contraception. Muramatsu suggests 70–75 percent abortion and 30–25 percent sterilization responsible for the fertility decline in Japan between 1947 and 1957.[26] Monreal and Armijo estimate births averted 50 percent by abortion and 50 percent by contraception in Chile.[27] The reasoning behind these estimates is, however, not supplied.

To my knowledge, no one has attempted to estimate the relative effects of abortion and contraception on birth rates in the United States. A more accurate abortion figure than the current estimate of one-million-per-year, combined with more up-to-date contraceptive use figures (anticipated from the 1970 National Fertility Survey) would make this possible.

Reports of fertility declines have several shortcomings in common. Some fail to note the degree of declining fertility

prior to widespread access to legal abortion or to the introduction of a family planning program. Most suffer from lack
of appropriate controls; i.e., it is difficult to determine to what
extent fertility would have been reduced anyway, in the
absence of either liberalized abortion laws or the introduction
of a family planning program.

CONCLUSIONS

While more research is needed on the complex interrelationship of abortion and contraception, some tentative conclusions can be drawn:

1. Poor use of contraception, or use of poor contraception,
promotes abortion use.

2. Good use of contraception, or use of good contraception,
reduces abortion use.

3. Abortion is probably an essential, if undesirable, interim
measure between no fertility control at all and preventing
births by contraception; abortion should not be seen as the
preferred method; it can be used initially as an emergency
measure in the absence of contraceptives, and eventually as a
back-up measure when contraceptives are in general use.

4. While abortion is only one means by which a population
already wishing to limit family size can do so, its ready availability (legally, or with little fear of prosecution) probably
serves as a stimulant to its use.

## SUGGESTIONS FOR FUTURE RESEARCH

1. Bumpass and Westoff report that "of the women who
originally desired only two children but have borne three or
more children, four-fifths report their last pregnancy as
unplanned. Women who desire only two children achieve
their desired number very early in the childbearing years,
and consequently face a longer period of exposure to the risk
of unwanted births than do women desiring larger families.
One-third of these women experienced at least one accidental

pregnancy, but this is consistent with a reasonably high contraceptive efficacy of over .995 per fertile period over the average of seven years since the birth of their second child."[28]

What could the reduction in unwelcome births be if women had access to *total* fertility control; i.e., including legal abortion? As abortion laws in the United States are repealed or declared unconstitutional, the opportunity for such measurement will present itself. Since it would be desirable to be able to predict what the reduction could be before the laws are actually changed, we may make two assumptions:

a. In countries where abortions are widely available, most "unwanted" births do not occur. It may be that not only definitely "unwanted" births may then be eliminated, but also the gray zone of strong ambivalence as well; i.e., legal abortion could mean the difference between an "acceptable" three-child family and a "preferred" two-child family.

b. A substantial proportion of women who find themselves unwillingly pregnant would avail themselves of legal abortion were it available.

2. Comparative effects of abortion and contraception availability on illegitimacy rates should also be examined; when it becomes possible to terminate unplanned pregnancies legally, is there a greater reduction in illegitimacy than when a family planning program is introduced?

3. In the case of WEUP (willful exposure to unwanted pregnancy[29]), would access to after-the-fact termination result in preventing the birth, or would the woman reject the use of abortion as well; i.e., should the phenomenon be labeled WEUP or WEUC (willful exposure to unwanted childbirth)?

4. The question of availability of contraception or abortion is not merely one of comparing the former with the latter; it is also a matter of comparative availability of either to certain subgroups in the population. In research on utili-

zation, we must ask abortion/contraception for whom, where, under what circumstances.

Requeña's model for class/time variations in reliance on abortion and contraception suggests research for others to determine the extent to which his model is applicable. Further analysis of abortion and contraceptive use by certain characteristics is indicated; e.g., Negro-white differentials in the United States, ethnic variations in eastern Europe, class, residence, and age differentials, etc.

5. It is often not clear whether use of contraception precedes abortion or whether abortion promotes the use of contraception. It is most important that further research be done on individual reproductive histories.

6. The relationship between abortion and contraception might be entirely different were knowledge of one or the other to be increased. We now know something of contraceptive knowledge but almost nothing about abortion knowledge; the latter should be included in KAP surveys.

Knowledge questions in future studies should probe the woman's familiarity with methods employed and her knowledge of where to look if she wanted an abortion.

7. To our knowledge, there exists no attitude surveys comparing women's feelings toward both contraception and abortion per se. Women should be asked which they would prefer under what circumstances; their preferences would then have to be examined in relation to their levels of knowledge regarding both procedures.

8. Physicians' attitudes are vital to the implementation of either a contraceptive program or a permissive abortion law. In addition to examining relative fees to the physician for delivery, abortion, and contraceptive care, physicians should be asked their attitudes toward all three. Most opinion surveys determine only the physicians' position on abortion law reform or repeal.

9. Fees to the physician are just one aspect of the relative "cost" of abortion and contraception to determine why one,

rather than the other, is utilized; we should also examine the cost to the woman (economic and psychological) and the cost to society (economic and social).

10. While some studies have been conducted to examine the psychological and social cost of abortion and nonabortion, and some of the psychological aspects, such as libido changes and willful exposure to unwanted pregnancy, and social aspects, such as illegitimacy and decreased fertility and its effects on changing life styles, of the use or nonuse of contraception, these have not so far been conducted on a comparative basis. A suggested "starter set" for some comparisons of outcomes might be the following:

|  | **Possible Consequences** | |
| --- | --- | --- |
| **Alternatives** | **Psychological** | **Social** |
| **Use contraceptives** | freedom from fear of pregnancy <br> guilt, remorse, regret | lower birth rate <br> aging population <br> fewer abortions <br> health care required |
| **Don't use contraceptives** | fear of pregnancy <br> guilt from abortion <br> pressures from delivery and child bearing | higher birth rate <br> higher abortion rate <br> welfare services for excess fertility |
| **Use abortion** | guilt, remorse, regret <br> free from unwanted child | cost of services and facilities <br> lower birth rate |
| **Don't use abortion** | unwanted child | welfare services for excess fertility <br> infanticide |

11. Psychological studies particularly suffer from considerable social context bias, and the difficult problem of adequate controls. Many examine only the *post*abortal state of dissatisfaction, guilt, or remorse. Those which do include the pre-abortion or prepregnancy state of the aborting woman are not designed to compare the short- or long-term consequences of abortion vs. delivery and child-rearing.

12. A further cost to the woman and to society is medical

sequelae. Tietze has provided a model comparing mortality costs.[30] We must also examine nonfatal sequelae and compare risks entailed in the use of orals, IUDs, abortion, and pregnancy. Women will make choices based on their limited knowledge of other women's side-effects from taking pills, or pelvic infections and uterine perforations with IUDs, and will compare them to what they know of abortion risks.

13. In assessing the medical capacity to handle abortions, the number of practicing obstetricians and gynecologists, number of deliveries, and number of present hospital admissions and bed-days for abortions and deliveries should be a noted and anticipated load in the event of a liberalization of the law.

14. The physician and psychiatrist offer us one perspective by reports on small series of patients, examined in depth; demographers and statisticians provide us another perspective —birth rates up or down, abortions up or down. But there are more social aspects of the abortion/contraception question which deserve the attention of social scientists.

For example, the economist can tell us not only what the trade-offs are of education costs and agricultural development vs. costs of family planning programs, but can also tell us something of the cost to society of providing full contraceptive care, and of providing delivery services and a variety of services for welfare, illegitimate, and other unplanned and/or unwanted births.

15. What can the anthropologist tell us? Apart from additions to the list of gruesome methods of accomplishing abortion, he can tell us that certain pregnancies not only can be but must be terminated in certain societies; this information throws the problem in a different light and gives us comparative societal norms by which to view our own attitudes and practices.

For instance, what do we know about American Indian attitudes and behavior? If abortions were to be made available in Indian Hospitals, would they respond with charges of genocide or would such a service be seen as a normal part of health care? Or would the response vary by tribe? We ought to know.

16. It's a pity to report that the sociologist's concern with abortion has been almost exclusively an interest in attitude surveys. The sociologist has found out a great deal about fertility behavior and about contraceptive knowledge, attitudes, and practice, but abortion has been almost entirely ignored. Kantner and Zelnick found that among a group of Negro women assembled to discuss fertility behavior, the topic of abortion was not volunteered, and when suggested by the moderator, was greeted with a strongly negative reaction; later the same women spoke approvingly of "bringing on a late period."[31] This tells us something about attitudes and behavior and helps us to formulate our questions.

17. We might also take a look at infant mortality figures and explore the problem of unconscious infanticide, as Viel has done in Chile.

18. We need better analysis of abortion data than merely $x$ percent were under 20, $y$ percent were 20 to 24, and so on. It is interesting to note, for instance, whether the investigator classifies women as ever married vs. never married, or currently married vs. currently not married. That is, what to do with the widowed, single or divorced (and consensual unions, concubines, etc.) might tell us something about the investigator's *own* attitude toward the subject's sexual activities.

19. The political scientist—or the political sociologist—can also contribute. There has been a gradual change in social/political climate regarding contraception, but we are witnessing a sudden change with respect to abortion. At the least we need a historian to chart the events. All of us can make informed guesses about the dynamics of social change, but I would prefer better analysis than my own informed guesses. The dynamics of the change, the pressure groups, the individuals, the lines of influence, should be examined. We used to hear that a large Catholic population meant death to a

family planning program; was that the political reality? Is the noninvolvement of the black community due to noninterest? Are efforts concentrated elsewhere? Or is there a strong anti-abortion feeling (Westoff, Moore, and Ryder found Negro views less liberal than white views).[32] What about the geno-cide issue—how deeply has it penetrated the black commu-nity? Is there a single antiabortion, anticontraception feeling, or are they separate and distinct?

20. Although it is of academic interest to know the opti-mum balance of abortion and contraception, it is of little use unless there is a realistic possibility for the allocation of funds, allowing so much for abortion and so much for contraception. That is, it would not seem worthwhile to designate as top priority a research undertaking to determine how many abortions would be needed to have x effect, and what their cost would be compared to that of providing contraception, if there is not even a remote possibility of the findings' being implemented in the country under study.

21. It should also be noted that when oral abortifacients become available, many of the comparisons between abortion and contraception which we now propose to study will be altered.

22. Funds should be made available for the translation of entire reports in foreign languages (not just tables), wherein a wealth of valuable data lie, inaccessible to most English-speaking researchers.

23. Every piece of research is a pilot study. Researchers should consider the opportunities for replicating others' case studies, in addition to contributing original approaches.

24. A systematic index of research findings, which would go beyond current abstracting services, should be designed in order to prevent duplication and to provide baseline informa-tion for new research. Legal indices provide guides to prece-dents, confirmations, and reversals; an abortion index might classify research findings in a similar manner.

## NOTES

1. Tietze, C., "Mortality with contraception and abortion," *Studies in Family Planning*, 45:6–8 (September 1969).

2. Westoff, C.; Moore, E. C.; and Ryder, N., "The structure of attitudes toward abortion," *Milbank Memorial Fund Quarterly*, 47(pt. 1):11–37 (January 1969).

3. Girard, A., and Zucker, E., "Une enquete auprès du public sur la structure familiale et la prévention des naissances," *Population*, 22:439–454 (May–June 1967).

4. Moore, E. C., and Dobson, L., Based on data collected in survey sponsored by The Population Council.

5. Taeuber, I., *The Population of Japan* (Princeton: Princeton University Press, 1958).

6. Potts, M., Talk at Planned Parenthood—World Population (New York: October 1969) (unpublished).

7. "News and notes," *British Medical Journal*, 3:245 (July 26, 1969).

8. Eliot, J.; Hall, R.; Willson, R.; and Houser, C. "The medical aspects of abortion: the obstetrician's view," *Abortion in a Changing World* (ed. R. E. Hall), 1:85–95 (New York: Columbia University Press, 1970).

9. Hubinont, P.; Brat, T.; Polderman, J.; and Ramdoyal, R., "The global aspects of abortion: abortion in western Europe," *Abortion in a Changing World* (ed. R. E. Hall), 1:325–337 (New York: Columbia University Press, 1970).

10. Glass, D. V., "Fertility and birth control in developed societies, and some questions of policy for less developed societies," *(Proceedings of the Seventh Conference* (International Planned Parenthood Federation) (Amsterdam: Excerpta Medica International Congress Series No. 72, 1963), pp. 38–46.

11. Hubinont *et al.*, "Abortion in western Europe."

12. Bachi, R., "The global aspects of abortion: abortion in Israel," *Abortion in a Changing World* (R. E. Hall, ed.), 1:274–283 (New York: Columbia University Press, 1970); Hutchinson, B., "Induced abortion in Brazilian married women," *America Latina*, 7:21–33 (October–December 1964); Chow, L. P.; Freedman, R.; Potter, R. G.; and Jain, A. K., "Correlates of IUD termination in a mass family planning program: the first Taiwan IUD follow-up survey," *Milbank Memorial Fund Quarterly*, 46 (pt. 1):215–235 (April 1968); The Population Problems Research Council, *Fifth Opinion Survey on Birth Control in Japan*, Population Problems Series No. 16 (Tokyo: Mainichi Newspapers, 1959), pp. 1–44; Hong, S., *Induced Abortion in Seoul, Korea* (Seoul: Dong-A Publishing Co., 1966), pp. 1–99.

13. Chow, et al., "First Taiwan IUD follow-up," pp. 215–235; Jain, A., "Fetal wastage in a sample of Taiwanese women," *Milbank Memorial Fund Quarterly*, 47(pt. 1):297–306 (July 1969); Chow, L. P.; Huang, T. T.; and Chang, M. C., "Induced abortion in Taiwan, Republic of China: a preliminary report" (Taichung: Taiwan Population Studies Center, May 1968), pp. 1–27 (mimeographed); Janmejai, K., "Socio-economic aspects of abortion," *Family Planning News*, 4:55–57 (March 1963); Agarwala, S. N., "Abortion rate among a section of Delhi's population," *Medical Digest*, 30:1–7 (January 1962); Mohanty, S. P., "A review of some selected studies on abortion in India," *Demographic, Social and Medical Aspects of Abortion* (Bombay: Demographic Training and Research Center, 1968), pp. 57–73; Valaoras V., "Greece: postwar abortion experience," *Studies in Family Planning*, 46:10–16 (October 1969); Requeña, M., "Social and economic correlates of induced abortion in Santiago, Chile," *Demography*, 2:33–49 (1965); Populations Problems Research Council, *Birth Control in Japan*, pp. 1–44.

14. Hong, *Induced Abortion in Seoul, Korea*, pp. 1–99; Chow, et al., "Induced Abortion in Taiwan," pp. 1–27; Requeña, M., "Chilean programme of abortion control and fertility planning, present situation and forecast for the next decade" (United Nations: CELADE, 1969) (mimeographed).

15. Monreal, T., and Armijo, R., "Evaluation of the program for the prevention of induced abortion and for family planning in the city of Santiago" (Santiago: Universidad de Chile, 1968) (mimeographed).

16. Foreningen for Familieplanlaegning, "National report of Denmark," *Sex and Human Relations: Proceedings of the Fourth Conference of the Region for Europe, Near East and Africa* (International Planned Parenthood Federation, 1965), pp. 209–211.

17. Potts, M., "Legal abortion in eastern Europe," *Eugenics Review*, 59:232–250 (December 1967).

18. Gold, E., Personal communication.

19. Faundes, A., unpublished data.

20. Monreal, and Armijo, "Prevention of induced abortion and family planning in Santiago" (see note 15); Faundes, A.; Rodriguez-Galant, G.; and Avendaño, O., "The San Gregorio experimental family planning program: changes observed in fertility and abortion rates," *Demography*, 5:836–845(1969).

21. Chow et al., "First Taiwan IUD follow-up," pp. 215–235.

22. Koya, Y., *Pioneering in Family Planning: A Collection of Papers on the Family Planning Programs and Research Conducted in Japan* (Tokyo: Japan Medical Publishers, Inc., 1963), see especially Chapters 2, 3, and 6.

23. Monreal and Armijo, "Prevention of induced abortion and family planning in Santiago."

24. Requeña, "Chilean programme of abortion control and fertility planning" (mimeographed), p. 11.

25. Potter, R.G., "Birth intervals: structure and change," *Population Studies*, 17:155–166, (November 1963).

26. Muramatsu, M., "Changing Japan, rapid decline in the birth rate: abortions outnumber births," *Family Planning*, 7:3–8 (October 1958).

27. Monreal and Armijo, "Prevention of induced abortion. . ." (see note 15).

28. Bumpass, L., and Westoff, C., "The prediction of completed fertility," *Demography*, 6:445–454 (November 1969).

29. Lehfeldt, H., and Guze, H., "Psychological factors in contraceptive failure," *Fertility and Sterility*, 17:110–116 (January–February 1966).

30. Tietze, "mortality with contraception and abortion," pp. 6–8.

31. Kantner, J., and Zelnick, M., "Exploratory studies of Negro family formation: common conceptions about birth control," *Studies in Family Planning*, 47:10–13 (November 1969).

32. Westoff *et al.*, "Structure of attitudes toward abortion," pp. 11–37.

# Discussion

**Sheps:** The kind of question I would like to ask in a study of children whose mother's requests for abortion were denied is "what are the disabilities for the child and the mother and for the rest of the family in a situation in which an abortion was definitely requested and denied?" I would compare these children with those whose parents were so well organized that they knowingly stopped any form of contraceptive practice to have a planned child in contrast to those whose mothers became pregnant by accident, and, who, after becoming pregnant, wanted an abortion and did not get it.

The other point I should like to make concerns the rapid rise and fall in the birth rate in Romania following the reinstitution of restrictions in their abortion law. About six months after the law in Romania was made more restrictive, the birth rate rose from about 13 per 1,000 population in December 1966 to about 40 per 1,000 in September 1967 and remained at that level for several months before it came down to about 22 per 1,000 by December 1968. Although it is very possible, and even likely, that women in Romania found a substitute for the legal abortions that they had previously had, I would like to point out that there is another reason for the rise in the birth rate followed by a drop under similar circumstances.

In general, a population that has a low birth rate, even if it is the result of abortions performed early in pregnancy, has relatively few women pregnant at any one point in time, and

157

relatively more women who are susceptible to becoming pregnant. The effect of a restrictive amendment to the abortion law is an immediate and sharp increase in the number of births nine months later. However, since most women who conceive remain pregnant for the full term of the pregnancy plus the months before ovulation is resumed, they are removed from the pool of women susceptible to becoming pregnant. Consequently, the conception rate declines and is followed by a decline in the birth rate nine months later.

**Tietze:** We should all have noticed years ago that a sizable age bias exists in all statistics on abortion ratios by age, that is, the number of abortions per 1,000 live births or per 1,000 pregnancies. Most of these statistics are based on the age of the woman at the end of the pregnancy. A woman who conceives when she is between 19 years and three months and 19 years and nine months of age is still in her teens if and when she aborts. If she carries the pregnancy to term, she is in the 20 to 24 year age group at the time of the birth. Because of the rapid rate of increase in conceptions during the late teens, the ratio of abortions to births is changed considerably when ratios are computed on the basis of age at time of conception.

For Czechoslovakia, we compared data on age-specific ratios of induced abortion and spontaneous abortion to live births, using age at time of conception, with conventionally computed ratios. We found that the age-specific ratios of abortions were lower for conceptions in the teens and in the early twenties, compared with the conventionally computed ratios, while in all the other age groups, the bias was in the other direction. The difference was at its maximum toward the end of the childbearing period, when the women giving birth were in the 45 to 49 year age group while those who aborted were in the 40 to 44 year age group.

With regard to evidence on changes in the number of illegal abortions in eastern Europe and in Japan, hard and fast proof of a decline is impossible because the number of illegal abortions is not known, either before or after the liberalization of the laws. It has been claimed that a large proportion, if not all, of the increase in legal abortion, was due to the transfer from the illegal area to the legal area, but there is no doubt that some illegal abortions still occur. What is the evidence that illegal abortions have declined? One bit of evidence is the course of so-called "other" abortions, which combine spontaneous and illegal abortions admitted to hospitals for aftercare or because of complications. In terms of rates per population or per women of reproductive age, the rate of other abortions has gone down, but not very much. I believe the decline in illegal abortions has been masked by increased admissions to hospitals. It is true that improvements in hospital and medical services have resulted in a tendency to move patients into hospitals and to have deliveries in hospitals. The percentage of deliveries in hospitals was much greater in 1965 than in 1955 in both Hungary and Czechoslovakia, and this may well apply to abortions. Increasing restrictions on the private practice of medicine has also contributed to an increase in the use of hospitals. Another bit of evidence, which is perhaps more satisfactory, is the course of the death rate from abortions, which has shown a drop of approximately 50 percent in Hungary and 75 percent in Czechoslovakia during the years from just before to just after the abortion law was liberalized.

**Brackett:** India seems to be on the verge of passing a liberalized abortion law, comparable to the present British law, except that the abortion must be certified by one physician, rather than the two required under the British law. There are many problems associated with liberalizing abortions in India because their medical facilities are very limited. An important issue concerns the possibility of training paramedical personnel or midwives to perform abortions.

**Pohlman:** The medical profession in India is ultraconservative and also heavily clustered in cities. If the paramedical

personnel were to be used for abortions in the villages the
critical problem is that there would be no hospitals nearby,
especially in the more remote areas. The health center program in India has not been extended to all areas. Further,
even the family planning services that are available are not
being used.

**David:** There is one additional point relating to the use of
paramedical personnel which should be brought out. Midwives currently earn their living from the delivery of babies
and the only way they can be compensated for fewer babies
is to assist with abortions. This may mean that there will be
economic as well as psychological incentives for midwives to
do abortions.

For generations we have had unwanted children in our
society, and we, as social scientists, have overlooked this key
problem. What has been lacking is a comprehensive social
science approach, not only from the point of view of physicians, sociologists, and political scientists, but with concern
for its humanistic and statistical aspects. We must be aware
of the various forces in our society which impinge on the
problem under study and of how to analyze and understand
better what is actually happening. Our basic responsibility is
to discover what the various avenues and approaches to a
problem are. What can we learn from other societies that
might be profitably applied to our own? And how can we
bring the best experience from all quarters to bear on our
particular problems in the most salutary ways?

**Markush:** This is an extremely important time to do studies
in the United States because of the changing legal situation.
Many states that have recently changed their laws would have
been ideal for "before" studies. I think we cannot do a pure
randomized study of abortions obtained and denied, but we
can come close to it through epidemiologic studies. Some
states are changing their laws, without any dramatic changes
in the birth rates or in abortion rates, and we ought to be
studying them to find out why the changes are so small. One

kind of epidemiologic study that is very much needed is a
survey in selected states, chosen on the basis of what might
happen in the future or on a random basis assuming that
neither the future nor legal changes can be predicted. Studies
of the vital statistics of these states may be misleading, perhaps
because vital statistics are not good in many respects but they
are suggestive and can serve as guides for more definitive
studies.

We also need to do longitudinal studies, starting with school
children and with the very young teens about their attitudes
toward family life and family planning. I believe it is possible
to follow people over long periods of time, perhaps for as long
as fifteen years, and to find out how their attitudes, their
knowledge, and their behavior relate to what actually happens
to them later on in life.

**Moore:** When we look at the forces and influences of social
action and social change, we learn something not just about a
specific program, but also about the network of society and
what people's underlying motives are. I believe that studying
the forces of social change is a valid area for research.

**Brody:** I look at such an approach as essentially ecologic,
because it includes all the important elements of a system and
its changing values. An example is northern Brazil, where
contraception is really unacceptable, not because of Catholic
attitudes, but because the rate of infant mortality is so high
that the people have what is sometimes called a gambler's
mentality. They have as many children as possible to maxi-
mize the chance of a few of them surviving. If you are going
to study contraception and abortion, you must take into account value systems and the process of change in these systems,
which means consideration of every element of the ecologic
scheme.

**David:** If an instrument to measure the motivation for contraception could be designed, then it would be possible to
predict who will probably require an abortion and who will

not. This would also enable us to devise special counseling programs for people at various motivational levels.

**Wolf:** We spent one summer at The Johns Hopkins Ob–Gyn Clinic studying why people reject birth control. We found that in more than one-half the cases women stated that they had not received any birth control information. Yet the doctor thought that he had given it! There are serious problems in communication that require intensive study, especially in this crucial and sensitive area.

# SECTION IV
# SOCIOECONOMIC ASPECTS

# Socioeconomic Outcomes of Present Abortion Regulations and Practices

Charlotte Muller, Ph.D.*

ACCESS to the market for legal abortions at the present time is, in general, restricted to women of means who are able to procure private medical and psychiatric care in hospitals and, thus, to establish the basis for medically safe service with hospital amenities.[1] Meanwhile, their less affluent sisters are rarely able to receive medically equivalent care on the wards of public hospitals or as service patients in voluntary hospitals. These facts have been well documented for hospitals in New York City, New York State, and the United States, in reports showing differences in the ratio of abortions to deliveries for patients on ward compared with private services and similar differences between public compared with other hospitals.[2]

The far larger market for illegal abortions is also class-structured in that it is the nonpoor patient who can afford to travel by jet to a gray market area or to purchase the services of a qualified physician, although without hospital protection or amenities. The poor candidate is more likely to end up in the hands of a nonmedical practitioner or to make crude

* Professor, Center for Social Research, City University of New York, New York, New York.

attempts at self-induced abortion through chemical and physical means.

Imperfections in the market for legal as well as for illegal abortions are largely due to uneven access to knowledge of sources of supply, as well as to the suppliers themselves, for economic, social, and geographic reasons. The result is a lessening of consumer welfare and, in particular, a restriction on the option of couples to choose fertility levels consistent with their preferences for leisure, material goods, the company of children, and the education they consider suitable for their children.[3]

Unlike some other health services, not fully utilized by low-income groups, abortion appears to be a service whose utilization would greatly rise in the event of legalization. This has been demonstrated by the experience of countries which have broadened the legal grounds for abortion to include the health of the mother, as well as a threat to her life, and to admit socioeconomic considerations. States like Colorado, which have also liberalized their abortion laws, have had a similar experience.[4] A more liberalized law in Great Britain was followed by a shift in abortions from private auspices to National Health Service hospitals, as well as in an increase in the total number of legal abortions performed.[5]

The wider access to legal abortions would doubtlessly result in a decline in the resort to inferior substitutes, including attempts at self-induced abortion, with a resultant improvement in the maternal death rate among black and Puerto Rican women.[6] However, it is not certain that all the latent demand would be satisfied: some women would resent the lack of privacy of official procedures, review by a committee, and the like; some physicians would refuse to perform the operation; and some women would deny the reality of the pregnancy until late in its course, as they now do. The price of the service would still be a factor in utilization although it is not easy to assess the elasticity of demand while legal barriers still exist. Present barriers to legal abortion affect the ratio of unwanted to wanted children. Since low-income couples are, in general, less successful users of contraception, abortion as a means of maintaining desired family size is, thus, of relatively greater importance to them than it is to high-income couples.[7] However, so long as low-income couples continue to desire three or four children or more, they may not use the available means of birth prevention, and per capita income would thus remain low. In any event, a reduction in unwanted births will not, of itself, solve the problems of poverty, which require a variety of specific programs to deal with such factors as low job skills, deficient labor market organization, family health needs, and income maintenance problems.

Uncontrolled births may have a negative effect on the economic and social welfare of the family, for such reasons as the birth of a first child before the young couple is prepared for it; closely spaced subsequent births, which may affect the family's capacity to accept the new child; and failure to terminate family formation when a desired size has been reached.

Although the worsening of family well-being is the joint result of the limitations of the current state of the birth control field, such as inaccessibility, failure to utilize available techniques, and imperfections in methods, and of restrictive abortion policies, it would nevertheless be possible to avert negative outcomes by changed abortion policy alone.

## FAMILY CYCLE AND ECONOMIC LIFE

One of the important factors relating to the economic life of the family is the separation of the teenage male from the educational process. The mechanism and the evidence linking the family cycle and economic life have been impressively presented by Schorr.[8] Marriages among teenagers are frequently due to premarital pregnancy, forcing the young father to leave school without an opportunity to return. The result is poor bargaining power in the job market and job choices.

if any, in low-opportunity situations because of the combination of immediate necessity, lack of information, and low skills. Although marriages among the very young are less stable, statistically speaking, than marriages at a later age, the probability of a larger family is more closely associated with early age at marriage. Whether the family is separated or united, the burden of support prevents the young adult from experimenting with various types of work. And the family fails to accumulate capital for any decisive improvement in its circumstances, which would be made possible by, for instance, additional training.

Statistical support for this contention includes: (1) the high percent of premarital pregnancy in school-age marriages (one-third of all school-age marriages, 87 percent of marriages where both spouses were high school students); (2) the larger family size for both white and black mothers who marry at 18 compared with those who marry two or three years later in life (white, 3.7 children compared with 2.8 children; black, 4.3 compared with 4.0). This comparison also reveals the limited success of black families at birth control, with age at marriage having less effect on family size than among white families; (3) the unfavorable occupational distribution of teenage males compared with older workers.[9] In 1966, of the 1.2 million young males 16 to 21 years of age who were school dropouts and members of the labor force, 61 percent were operatives or nonfarm laborers.[10]

The economic history of the teenage married male is characterized by the reduced lifetime earnings of a man who has not completed high school and the lesser earnings of the high school graduate compared with the college graduate. Estimates for 1967 show a lifetime income for males 25 years and older by years of schooling as follows: 1–3 years of high school, $275,000; 4 years of high school, $325,000; 4 or more years of college, $529,000.[11]

Differences can also be observed in a cross-section of two educational levels tabulated by ethnic group. The median income for 1966 was $11,697 for 5.8 million white family heads who were college graduates, compared with a median income of $7,267 for 7.9 million family heads who did not finish high school. For nonwhite families, comparable figures were $9,510 (235,000 families) and $4,418 (1.1 million families), respectively.[12]

These income figures would be affected by changes in the relative supply of males at different educational levels and also by changes in the structure of the demand for workers at different occupational levels. Nevertheless, the return on human capital from additional education is both real and realizable. It is estimated that four-fifths of the high school dropouts are intellectually capable of additional education.[13]

Another barrier to the economic improvement of the family relates to job-seeking by the mature woman with children. The median family income in 1966 was more than one-fourth higher for families with a male head when the wife was in the paid labor force than when she was not.[14] The presence of children under six is a deterrent to the mother's labor force participation.[15] Although it is true that such women are generally young and untrained and may not add greatly to family resources by being employed, what is implied is that training programs are needed to capitalize on the economic opportunity presented to the family by the mother's freedom from pregnancy. In many communities girls who become pregnant are compelled to leave school, thus, adding to the negative effect on the long-run family earning potential described above for teenage males. Girls who started their families in their teens join the ranks of women with little or no training for the labor market when they reach maturity. Finally, for married women with young children who must work out of financial necessity (about one-half of those who took jobs in 1963), unsatisfactory or no arrangements for child care may represent the price paid by the family for the mother's labor force participation, and the reason for the fluctuations in her availability for work.[16] To a considerable degree, the same conditions apply to middle-class women who wish to work for personal satisfaction and extra income.

The availability of the young widow for employment is to an extent dictated by the age of her youngest child and the number of her children, as it is for the married woman. Half of the widowed mothers with three or more children did not work at all in 1962, compared with 28 percent of those with only one child, and the other half tended to work only part-time. Since part-time employment is usually available in lower-paying occupations, their earning power was reduced by both time and occupational factors. Furthermore, employment and earnings after termination of child-care benefits under social security are found to be greatly affected by the woman's work experience in the preceding five years. Hence, the economic potential of young widows is greatly influenced by the size and spacing of their families.[17]

A third economic problem exacerbated by uncontrolled family size is present poverty. Orshansky points out: "The family with 5 or more children was still (in 1966) $3\frac{1}{2}$ times as likely to be poor as the family raising only one or two, and . . . almost half the poor children were in families with 5 or more children." She further points out that large families (four or more children) were found among an increasing number of poor families with a fully employed head (37 percent in 1965). How poor is poor? The median income of a poor family with a male head in 1966 was $3,308 for a four-child family, $3,590 for a five-child family, and $3,440 for a family of six or more children.[18]

About one-fourth of poor families, and about one-fifth of near-poor families, (or 2,244,000 out of 15,240,000 families in the poor and near-poor categories in 1966) had four or more children.[19] The family income figures for the large poor family are equivalent to a per capita income of $552, $513, and $430 (or less), respectively. In sharp contrast, the lowest budget standard for a four-person urban family as priced by the Bureau of Labor Statistics (BLS) in 1967, was $5,915 or $1,479 per capita.[20]

The immediate consequence of spreading fixed family resources over more persons is fewer goods and services per capita. Transfer payments received by about one-fourth of the poor (assistance, social security payments, veterans' pensions, and other devices to transfer current national income between persons by the tax-spending mechanism) are already included in current income. Even with public assistance, the large poor family cannot hope to consume at anywhere near the lowest budget standard of the BLS.

## UNWANTED CHILDREN

Children who lack a welcoming and nurturing parental home can be classified along a continuum which includes adoption, foster home placement, court action for neglect and dependency, and a less severe but indifferent or otherwise unsatisfactory parental role performance within the family of origin. To count the numbers involved is to become cognizant of the vast numbers of children affected by the various degrees and causes of being unwanted during childhood, although one cannot always infer that the child was unwanted during the pregnancy. The program costs involved, as in foster care or in institutional care, must be reduced by the amount of the maintenance component, which would be incurred (although not necessarily at the same level) regardless of where a child is raised. However, program costs would be higher if services, such as schooling or needed health care for pregnant girls, were more adequate.

The number of out-of-wedlock births is often one measure of the problem related to unwantedness. In 1967, there were 318,072 out-of-wedlock births, and the figure is expected to reach 403,000 by 1980, corresponding to a rate of 24 per 1,000 unmarried women 15–44 years of age. Forty-seven percent of these births are to girls under 20 years of age.[21] In 1966, births to unwed mothers represented 8.4 percent of all live births.[22] Since out-of-wedlock births are occasionally not unwanted and some are followed by marriage, the number of unwanted births may overstate the problem.[23] However, it should also be borne in mind that many births among married women are undesired as well as unplanned. One even finds children placed for adoption whose parents are living together. Children born after the pregnancy has been followed by marriage may be found among the adopted as well as among those who remain with their parents.

Another figure cited in connection with the measurement of the problem of unwanted children is the number offered for adoption. This group totalled 158,000 in 1967, or 82.3 per 10,000 children under five years of age, but only two-thirds of these were out-of-wedlock births.[24] Extra-legal but permanent adoptions add to these figures.

Many children are not adoptable because of a handicap or retention of parental rights, sometimes by incompetent parents, or because of racial or religious prejudice. Yet adoptions certainly provide a minimum estimate of the occurrence of unwanted births which could have been prevented.

Birth order is not necessarily related to unwantedness. A wealthy family can provide for a fourth or fifth child both materially and with personal care. A poor family, or one where the mother has a health impairment, may not be able to welcome a third child. Nevertheless, birth order, especially in conjunction with income level, is a useful measure of the problem of preventable births. Orshansky's figures yield a count of at least 2.2 million fourth children among the poor and near-poor, 1.3 million fifth children, and .7 million sixth children.[25] These figures may be contrasted with average family size preferences of 2.9 children for nonwhite families and 3.3 for white families.

It may be pointed out here that in a study of cases of severe parental neglect the average family size was eight people. Families guilty of child neglect were described as having inadequate diet, irregular meals, and poor food preparation; lack of cleanliness, absence of routine; and neglect of medical problems. Apathy was the predominant trait. Both internal and external means for building a positive life style were lacking. The children were often in trouble in school.[26]

The possibility of identifying unwanted children by comparing family size goals with actual family size depends on the time at which these goals were ascertained. Couples may adapt their announced goals in the event of pregnancy (and a portion of them even succeed in adapting their attitude and behavior).[27] Conversely, a child originally desired may become unwanted because of the likelihood of deformity, the death or disability of a parent, change in income, or the breakup of the marriage. This change in status has a bearing on the question of abortion only insofar as it occurs soon after conception.

If correct, the comparison of desired with actual family size is a powerful measure. It reveals between 750,000 and 1 million excess births a year between 1960 and 1965. These figures are based on a reanalysis of 1965 national survey data. The lower estimate is based on births unwanted by both parents, and the higher, on births unwanted by at least one parent. If one uses the higher estimate, 445,000 or 42 percent of all births among the poor and near-poor are unwanted, compared with 17 percent among the nonpoor. The incidence of unwanted births increases rapidly with birth order. The estimates cited are minimal because some births are retrospectively rationalized by the parents, and all births representing timing failures are omitted.[28]

Children whose early years are spent under psychological rejection by their mothers, abandonment by their fathers, in extreme poverty, and under other disadvantaged conditions are exposed to the risk of impaired development which, regardless of all other consequences, is important as a cause of reduced earning power at maturity. In the several aspects of this problem to be discussed, it is suggested that it is chiefly, although by no means only, impaired education which threatens future economic potential.

## MENTAL RETARDATION AND MENTAL HEALTH

Seeking of prenatal care late in pregnancy and inadequate nutrition are frequent in unwanted pregnancies. At least for high-risk mothers, late care and poor diet are a factor in complications and prematurity, which, in turn, are found to be related to the impaired learning potential of the child. Pasamanick has pointed out that very young mothers and older women had a higher risk of producing mentally defective children, and that this risk also increased with birth order.[29] It has also been noted that the excess medical risks of pregnancy among the very young are increased by the unmarried status and poverty of the adolescent girl who finds herself in this situation.[30]

Although being unwanted is not necessarily a factor in mental retardation in the sense of being either a necessary or a sufficient cause, it is pertinent that of the many births among the poor exposed to the hazards which may lead to mental retardation, a large percent appear to be unwanted. Since mental retardation is a multi-caused phenomenon in which the nurture, educational stimulation, and social opportunities of the child affect outcome, it can be surmised that a mild handicap (the more typical case) is continually reinforced in the large, poor, culturally isolated family. Furthermore, once adolescence is reached, access to higher education and to responsible jobs is dependent on being in the upper track of learners. The chance to increase earning power either by adding to human capital or by access to expensive cooperating factors of production is impaired by mild mental retardation.

The mental health of an infant is said to be affected by the same considerations in the prenatal environment as apply to postnatal development of learning capacity. Pasamanick mentions five clinical entities in children significantly associated with complications of pregnancy and prematurity: cerebral palsy, epilepsy, mental deficiency, behavior disorders, and

reading disabilities. "Cases" differ from controls not in operative procedures or in long and difficult labor but in protracted
toxemias and bleeding; i.e., in medical rather than obstetrical
features. Summing up, Pasamanick states: "There exists a continuum of reproductive insult, at least partially socioeconomi-
cally determined, resulting in a continuum of reproductive
casualty extending from death through varying degrees of
neuropsychiatric disability."[31]

Acceptance by and the interaction with parents continues
to be an influential factor in the course of mental health
throughout childhood.[32]

In a study of cases of children requiring agency foster care
in New York City, 10 percent of initial placements were due
to severe neglect or abuse, and 33 percent to family problems
including rejection milder than the preceding category.[33] An
annual figure of 154,000 juvenile court cases of dependency
or neglect, corresponding to a rate of 2.1 per 1,000 children,
in jurisdictions covering two-thirds of the population under
18 years of age, is said to be an understatement of the incidence of this problem.[34]

Impaired mental health interferes with the formal educational process, sometimes manifested by behavior problems in
the classroom, and with socialization of the child, impeding
his performance in the labor market at the maximum level of
his capacities. At its worst, delinquency, incarceration, or
other socially punitive responses remove him from the conventional development sequence. It has been observed that
delinquents often come from broken homes or have many
brothers and sisters; a correlation has also been noted between
adolescent misbehavior and the absence of the father or
limited opportunity to identify with him.[35] There were about
700,000 cases of juvenile delinquency in 1967, or 2.3 percent
of children between 10 and 17 years of age, and the rate
appears to be rising.[36]

The educational growth of children in the large families
where income and parental time are inadequate is often im-

paired. Income may be a substitute for time, as when the
mother reads to the four-year-old while a sitter walks the
baby, or when the four-year-old is sent to a private nursery
school while the mother tends the baby. This problem is far
broader than actual mental retardation or diagnosed mental
illness.[37]

Finally, the large poor family is less likely to secure medical
attention for its children.[38] The number of school days lost
because of illness is greater than it is for higher income
groups.[39] Nutrition deficiencies extend the time necessary for
recovery after infection and also affect the number of days of
school missed. Continuous school attendance has significance
for human development.

## SUMMARY

It is difficult to assign a weight to the importance of births
in excess of desired family size, or births ill-timed in terms of
family welfare, in the creation of such social problems as
child neglect, delinquency, and psychological and social in-
capacity to care for children. Nor is it easy to isolate the effects
of this factor on the set of job vs. education choices made by
the young father, the difficulties faced by the older woman in
planning reentry into the labor market, and the experience
of being a child consumer at the poverty level of income.
Equally, the underdevelopment of human capital because of
mental retardation, physical and psychiatric health problems,
and educational and nutritional undernourishment defies
exact division among specific causes. However well research
methods for dealing with multi-caused phenomena may succeed in elucidating these relationships in the future, there is
in any event food for thought in the present. Ability to control family size, including the right to abortion, must essentially seek approval on its merits: personal freedom, equal
access to care, and medical protection of the poor are all
involved. Yet the discussion cannot help being influenced by

observed associations between unplanned births and poverty, untimely marriage, and creation of stress on parental capacities of the more vulnerable for whatever reason.

## FUTURE RESEARCH

The design of relevant research concerning access to, and financing of, abortion services calls for flexibility because of the fluid situation which now exists with respect to law and practice. If realistic, such research can be useful in guiding policy choices.

1. Financial needs of patient groups can be identified by studying total service costs under varying marital, social, racial, and medical-clinical situations of the patient. Women who have had illegal abortions appear to be more willing than it was previously assumed to reveal information on incidence, prevalence, and attendant circumstances.[40] This may make it possible to develop estimates of direct costs for medical care and associated travel, and for the indirect costs of lost work time and child care, both on a per case basis and for total numbers. Such data can be used to supplement hospital records of postabortion morbidity and routine reports of puerperal deaths due to abortion, from which estimates of direct and indirect costs due to morbidity and mortality can be made. There should be fewer difficulties in assembling cost information for legal procedures.

The present cost of pregnancy tests, surgery, and hospital days, determined by current methods of medical care research, can serve as a guide to the program expenditures that would be necessary to assure economic access for the low-income woman as state laws on abortion are revised or repealed.

2. Systematic observation of the medical and behavioral effects on the woman of nonhospital service programs, and of their use of manpower and space resources, could be carried out as such programs are mounted, to aid in developing and revising standards for nonhospital services.

3. Understanding of items 1 and 2 above is essential for the design of an adequate prepayment benefit; this task needs to be supported by a survey of present coverage and gaps. Insurance entitlements for maternity benefits in the private sector vary widely by employment group and carrier. Nevertheless, an estimation of current practices as to waiting periods, in-hospital care requirements, schedule limits, and family contract conditions is needed. Public sector entitlements have their own sources of geographical and program variation within programs for military dependents, welfare, and Office of Economic Opportunity (OEO) medical care.

4. Finally, estimation of manpower needs is crucial in view of the unmet demand. The assessment of additional training required to prepare practicing physicians and medical students to participate in the provision of abortion services is one task. The appraisal of the attitude of professionals focuses on an element as important as the number of adequately trained personnel. The possible role of paraprofessionals is a related theme for health manpower research. This is especially interesting because the health field has before it the task of creating what is virtually a new service where traditional guild issues may be somewhat subdued.

States which have liberalized their abortion laws constitute a natural laboratory for the trial of new approaches in regard to financing, organization, manpower, and referral. Although little advantage has yet been taken of this fact, evaluation of early experience should be encouraged to aid in the development of appropriate social mechanisms for service.

## NOTES

1. Editorial, "Abortion and the Law," *Journal of the American Medical Association*, 199:179–180 (January 16, 1967).

2. Hall, R. E., "Present abortion practices in hospitals of New York State," *New York Medicine*, 23:124–126 (March 1967); Hall, "Therapeutic abortion, sterilization, and contraception," *American Journal of Obstetrics and Gynecology*, 91:518–532 (February 1965).

3. Easterlin, R. A., "Toward a socioeconomic theory of fertility: survey of recent research on economic factors in American fertility," *Fertility and Family Planning* (ed. S. J. Behrman; L. Corsa, Jr.; R. Freedman), 127–156 (Ann Arbor: University of Michigan Press, 1969).

4. Ayd, F. J., Jr., "Liberal abortion laws," *America,* 120:130–132 (February 1, 1969).

5. Tietze, C., "Legal abortion in industrialized countries," *Population Control* (ed. N. Sadik; J. K. Anderson; K. A. Siddigi; B.U.D. Ahmad, M. N. Butt; S. Samad; K. Sharih) (Islamabad: Pakistan Family Planning Council, 1969), pp 213–234.

6. Gold, E. M.; Erhardt, C. L.; Jacobziner, H.; Nelson, F. C., "Therapeutic abortions in New York City: A 20-year Review," *American Journal of Public Health,* 55:964–972 (July 1965).

7. Jaffe, F. S., and Guttmacher, A. F., "Family planning programs in the United States," *Demography,* 5:910–928 (1968).

8. Schorr, A. L., "The family cycle and income development," *Social Security Bulletin,* 29:14–26 (February 1966).

9. *Ibid.*

10. United States: Department of Commerce, *Statistical Abstract of the United States* (Washington, D.C., 1968), p. 114.

11. *Ibid.,* p.108.

12. *Ibid.,* p. 327.

13. United States: Children's Bureau, *The Nation's Youth: A Chart Book,* Publication No. 460 (Washington, D.C., 1968), Chart 28 and text.

14. United States: Department of Commerce, *Statistical Abstract of the United States* (Washington, D.C., 1968), p. 328.

15. ———, *United States Census of Population 1960 Labor Reserve* (Washington, D.C., 1966), PC(2) 6C, Table 14.

16. United States: Department of Labor, *Why Women Start and Stop Working: A Study in Mobility,* Special Labor Force Report No. 59 (Washington, D.C., September 1965), p. 1078.

17. United States: Social Security Administration, *Some Facts about the Employment of Widowed Mothers,* Research and Statistics Note No. 15, 1969 (Washington, D.C., August 20, 1969).

18. Orshansky, M., "The shape of poverty in 1966," *Social Security Bulletin,* 31:3–31 (March 1968).

19. *Ibid.*

20. United States: Department of Labor, *3 Standards of Living for an Urban Family of Four Persons,* Bulletin No. 1570–1575 (Spring 1967) (Washington, D.C., 1969), p. 6.

21. National Council on Illegitimacy, *Comments on Recent Trends in Illegitimacy in the U. S.* (New York, June 13, 1969), pp. 1–3 (mimeographed).

22. United States: Department of Commerce, *Statistical Abstract of the United States* (Washington, D.C., 1968), pp. 50–51.

23. Sauber, M., and Rubenstein, E., *Experiences of the Unwed Mother as a Parent* (New York: Community Council of Greater New York, 1965), pp. 152–153.

24. United States: Department of Commerce, *Statistical Abstract of the United States* (Washington, D.C., 1968), p. 10; United States: Children's Bureau, *Supplement to Child Welfare Statistics—1967*, Statistical Series 92 (Washington, D.C., 1968), pp. 1, 11.

25. Orshansky, "Shape of poverty in 1966," pp. 3–31.

26. Young, L. R., "An interim report on an experimental program of protective service," *Child Welfare*, 45:374–377 (July 1966).

27. United States: Social Security Administration, "Economic status, unemployment, and family growth," *Social Security Bulletin*, 30:39–42 (May 1966).

28. Bumpass, L., and Westoff, C. F., "The perfect contraceptive population: extent and implications of unwanted fertility in the U. S.," Paper presented at Planned Parenthood-World Population (New York, N. Y., October 28, 1969), pp. 1–29 (mimeographed).

29. Pasamanick, B., "Epidemiological investigations of some prenatal factors in the production of neuropsychiatric disorders," *Health and the Community* (ed. A. H. Katz and J. S. Felton) (New York: Free Press, 1965), pp. 1–877.

30. United States: Children's Bureau, *Childbearing in and Before the Years of Adolescence* (Washington, D.C., 1967), pp. 3, 10.

31. Pasamanick, "Some prenatal factors in the production of neuropsychiatric disorders."

32. Mulford, R. M., "Emotional neglect of children: a challenge to protective services," *Child Welfare*, 37:19–24 (October 1958); Greenberg, N. H., "Studying the infant-mother relationship for clues to the causes of aberrant development," *Mental Health Program Report No. 1* (Washington, D.C., February 1967), pp. 255–265.

33. Jenkins, S., and Sauber, M., *Paths to Child Placement* (New York City Department of Welfare, 1966), pp. 9, 24.

34. United States: Children's Bureau, *Juvenile Court Statistics 1967* (Washington, D.C., 1969), pp. 1, 6.

35. United States: National Institute of Mental Health, *The Mental Health of Urban America*, Public Health Service Publication No. 1906 (Washington, D.C., April 1969), pp. 12, 17, 32.

36. See note 34.

37. See note 35.

38. United States: National Center for Health Statistics, *Volume of*

*Physician Visits: United States—July 1966–June 1967*, Series 10, No. 49 (Washington, D.C.: November 1968), p. 6.

39. ———, *Disability Days: United States—July 1965–June 1966*, Series 10, No. 47 (Washington, D.C.), p. 7.

40. Lee, N. H., *The Search for an Abortionist* (Chicago: University of Chicago Press, 1969), pp. xv, 207.

# Discussion

Tietze: I would like to discuss the quantitative aspects of the unwanted child problem if some of the present trends continue. I assume that a large proportion, though not all illegal abortions, will be transferred to abortions performed through legal channels. In addition, the total number of abortions probably will increase for two reasons: (1) I assume that the laws have had some deterrent effect in the past; and (2) it is also likely that the quantity and quality of contraception will be reduced, resulting in an increase in conceptions and, therefore, a greater need for pregnancy interruption. According to the National Fertility Survey of 1965, approximately 5 million unwanted births occurred in the six years immediately preceding the survey. In the forseeable future, therefore, it is likely that a sizable proportion of these unwanted pregnancies, perhaps one-half or about 2.5 million, may be aborted.

To anticipate a doubling or a near doubling of the total number of induced abortions in the United States is realistic and should be in the back of our minds in visualizing the consequences. I believe that even 2 million abortions performed under safe conditions are far less threatening to life and health, physical and mental, than one million abortions performed under present-day clandestine conditions. However, it is essential that the order of magnitude of the consequences should be kept in mind by persons concerned with planning for research and services.

**Matory:** I should like to propose a study to determine how, by whom, and under what conditions contraceptives should be provided to teenage children, especially the very young, sexually active teenager. Abortion may be the back-up technique, but younger persons need other equally important forms of service, such as sex and family life education.

**Wolf:** Counseling and service to adolescents should take place through schools because that is where you find them. However, most of the schools have been reluctant or poorly equipped to approach this subject. A project jointly sponsored by the Planned Parenthood Federation of America, the Ford Foundation, and The Johns Hopkins School of Hygiene and Public Health is under way in three census tracts in west Baltimore. The study is trying to discern the life style of adolescents. Part of the study has turned into an information service for people who want help but do not know where to get it.

With regard to changing abortion laws and their effects, I am reminded of our experience at Johns Hopkins in relation to the "sex change" program. The Gynecology Department was instrumental in assisting the Blue Cross-Blue Shield to approve sex change as a payable surgical procedure. However, it entailed a long process of negotiation, but it may serve as a precedent in aiding Blue Cross and other carriers to extend themselves to new areas.

**Muller:** It is a question of economic bargaining and not of political strategy. So long as the laws under which the programs are incorporated do not specifically prohibit the action, it is a matter of encouraging member groups to negotiate and exert pressure for an expanded coverage.

**Tietze:** There has been considerable disagreement about whether most abortions are provided for married or single women. The higher the legal abortion rate in a country the lower is the proportion of unmarried women among those aborted. The proportion is lowest in Hungary, Czechoslovakia and highest in the United States. Apparently, in the cultural setting in which we operate, when abortion is not readily available, greatest pressure is exerted on the unmarried girl and her parents.

In the report of the Danish Abortion Commission published last year, the predominant diagnoses for married women were what is described as "stress neurosis" and neurasthensia, but among the unmarried, it was depressive reaction, implying suicidal tendencies.

**Wolf:** In the Danish Report, it was also pointed out that only 3 percent of the unwed mothers released their children for adoption, which is a far different situation from the one in this country.

**Pohlman:** One might speculate that the higher the motivation for abortion the more hurdles one is willing to surmount in order to get it. Women who become pregnant out of wedlock in countries which frown on such conceptions are more strongly motivated, so when abortion is difficult to obtain, the result is that the most highly motivated women surmount the hurdles and obtain the abortions in one or another way.

# Appendix A

## LIST OF MAJOR RESEARCH PROPOSALS*

I. MORTALITY AND MORBIDITY

1. Develop standards for: (a) definitions of such terms as abortions—induced, spontaneous, septic, early and late, complications and sequelae—mild and severe, early and late; (b) criteria for mortality from abortion; (c) indications for abortion; (d) effects of abortions granted and denied; (e) terminology for use in measuring frequency of abortion; (f) reporting periods of gestation and types of operations; (g) determination of completeness of reporting.

2. Analyze the records of obstetrical departments in teaching centers and large hospitals where abortions are performed under current laws and practices for the purposes of: (a) describing the present status of abortion in terms of numbers, administrative and medical procedures employed in various jurisdictions, characteristics of women who are aborted compared with those who are not, and other variables; (b) producing indicators of what might be expected medically and clinically under conditions of expanding abortion requirements with a view to assessing the practicability and safety of outpatient procedures; (c) presenting the findings and experiences of physicians on pathology associated with different abortion techniques correlated with varying periods of gestation; (d) evaluating the public health problem as indi-

* Prepared with the assistance of Mrs. Edna Unger.

187

cated by hospital admissions for complications, and by mortality, from illegally induced abortions by various characteristics of the woman; and (e) comparing early and late sequelae of abortions performed in hospitals with those done illegally, by various characteristics of the woman.

3. Conduct longitudinal studies of the reproductive, menstrual, and sexual functions of women who had had abortions to document (a) such factors as recidivism, and (b) possible late somatic outcomes, including secondary sterility, prematurity, ectopic pregnancy, and pelvic inflammatory disease.

4. Conduct short-term studies to determine possible early complications of abortions performed in hospitals by characteristics of the women, duration of pregnancy, type of procedure, and type of hospital service.

5. Investigate alternative systems of relevant medical service, including documentation of (a) safety, feasibility, and needed safeguards for outpatient abortions; (b) specification of situation requiring direct psychiatric examination of patients or consultation with colleagues; and (c) circumstances under which paramedical personnel may be advantageously used in the abortion process.

6. Develop safe, inexpensive time- and manpower-saving techniques for termination of early unwanted pregnancy, including self-administered pregnancy tests, postcoital pills, and simple abortion techniques, such as cryosurgery and electrolysis.

7. Establish methods and criteria for predicting which women will be benefited by abortion and which women will be at risk for harmful somatic, psychiatric, and social outcomes of performed and denied abortions.

8. Design a methodological study to: (a) determine the incidence of abortion by state, metropolitan area, city; (b) establish a floor for the incidence of abortions in the United States; (c) validate the reliability of information obtained.

9. Establish a surveillance system of maternal deaths, including pathological studies of all women who die between

the ages of 15 and 49 years; make follow-back studies of death certificates for younger women; compare mortality from abortion by socioeconomic characteristics of the woman.

10. Develop professional and public educational procedures to promote the earliest possible reporting and determination of unwanted pregnancy for the purpose of maximizing safety and reducing costs associated with abortion.


II. MENTAL HEALTH AND RELATED CONSIDERATIONS

1. Use a randomized series of in-depth interviews to develop standardized psychological scales so that abortion seekers could be grouped according to the principal emotional aspects involved and to the intensity of their feelings.

2. Conduct longitudinal studies of abortions granted or denied for the purpose of developing predictive measures for determining the characteristics of women, children, and families at risk of adverse mental health outcomes; and for predicting future attitudes of women toward childbearing.

3. Set up interview programs for women seeking abortion, prior to medical examination, to determine attitudes and emotions toward the abortion and compare with responses to same questions after a medical examination.

4. Study stability of atitudes toward pregnancy and/or abortion over time, setting up a Rejection Quotient based on a continuum of feelings of wantedness-unwantedness, and determine earliest point in time when Rejection Quotient can be measured; compare children of women whose requests for abortion were denied with a suitable control group.

5. Conduct epidemiological studies of the long-term effects of unwantedness on children and of unwanted children on families; develop measures of unwantedness; identify points in time of greatest risk of damaging consequences of unwantedness; linking psychiatric and epidemiological approach, determine changes in life cycle and social structure of those

affected by abortion; study effects of a woman's death on the structure and psychological composition of her family.

6. Compare groups of women matched for various demographic and socioeconomic characteristics to determine psychological and psychiatric sequelae of abortions granted and denied, and develop individual predictive measures based on group characteristics.

7. Identify the indications for psychiatric examination of the patient and for consultation; evaluate the purposes and usefulness of such examinations and consultations, from the standpoint of the obstetrician-gynecologist, the hospital committee, the pregnant woman and her family.

8. Enumerate and assess professional, ethical, and administrative problems of psychiatrist-patient relationships based on legal sanctions and unusual time pressures.

9. Compare women who cope with an unwanted pregnancy by: (a) seeking an abortion; (b) carrying the pregnancy to term but seeking or accepting long-range foster care or adoption; (c) carrying the pregnancy to term with the intention of rearing the child. Identify and assess the social factors that support or discourage the use of these options.

10. Identify the characteristics of women who succeed and those who fail to obtain abortions.

11. Conduct surveys to explore knowledge and attitudes of physicians and paramedical personnel concerning sexuality, delivery, contraception, abortion, and population problems.

12. Set up a register for psychiatrists to report every abortion requested and follow cases through all available agencies.

### III. ABORTION AND FAMILY PLANNING

1. Improve and refine techniques for measuring the incidence of legal and illegal abortions in the United States.

2. Study effect of changes in abortion laws on the numbers of unwanted conceptions and out-of-wedlock pregnancies and births, and on the use of contraception.

3. Document impact of educational programs and the changing legal and social status of abortion on knowledge, attitudes, and behavior of populations with regard to sexuality, contraception, abortion, and family life.

4. Maintain a historical chronicle and political analysis of the influence of social and political action groups and individuals on the changing social and legal climate with regard to abortions.

5. Study availability to specified populations of contraception and abortion in terms of demographic, socioeconomic, and geographic differentials.

6. Survey knowledge, attitudes, and practices (KAP) to elucidate relationship between contraception and abortion, including consumer-awareness of where to go and how to obtain service, and women's preferences as to use of contraception and abortion.

7. Prepare an inventory or handbook on abortion, containing relevant medical, behavioral, legal, social, demographic, and resource information on a national and international basis.

8. Index, translate, and disseminate foreign language reference materials on abortion.

9, Develop educational programs to enhance awareness and skill of physicians and ancillary personnel for dealing appropriately and adequately with abortion requests and related problems.

10. Develop a multidisciplinary instrument to improve the assessment of motivational factors involved in use of contraception vis a vis abortion.

11. Study the effect of contraceptive failures on use of abortion in relation to specific family planning programs.

12. Study the effect on induced abortion and on fertility rates of early postpartum or postabortum insertions of IUDs.

13. Develop follow-up procedures for assuring maintenance of contraceptive supplies for women receiving initial supply postabortum.

IV. SOCIOECONOMIC FACTORS

1. Develop methods of measuring direct and indirect costs of approved abortion in terms of medical care with and without complications, travel, lost work time, and child care, by marital, social, ethnic, and economic situation of the woman.

2. Review present provisions for maternity benefits and sick leave in private insurance and public programs, including practices as to waiting periods, in-hospital care, and family contract provisions; study feasibility of a prepayment insurance benefit program providing for coverage of pregnancy interruption.

3. Assess capacity to handle increasing numbers of abortions in the event that laws are liberalized or repealed, in terms of available obstetrician-gynecologists, hospital space, bed-days for in-hospital abortions, ambulatory service, and treatment of complications.

4. Identify financial needs of women grouped by social class in terms of availability of abortion and related services.

5. Develop measures of the indirect long-run cost of requested but denied abortions from the standpoint of the woman, her family, the unwanted child, and society.

6. Study the official and private channels through which women seek abortions in terms of efficiency and availability.

7. Study direct costs of various operative procedures for abortion, including surgical fees, hospital stay, and nursing care.

# Appendix B

## COCHAIRMEN, PARTICIPANTS, COMMENTATORS, AND OBSERVERS

**Cochairmen:**

Sidney H. Newman, Ph.D., Behavioral Scientist Administrator, Population and Reproduction Grants Branch, Center for Population Research, National Institute of Child Health and Human Development, Bethesda, Maryland.

Mildred B. Beck, M.S.W., Acting Chief, Office of Information, National Center for Family Planning Services, Health Services and Mental Health Administration, Bethesda, Maryland.

**Participants:**

John Asher, M.D., Epidemic Intelligence Officer, assigned to Department of Gynecology and Obstetrics, Emory University School of Medicine by Family Planning Evaluation Activity, Epidemiology Program, National Communicable Disease Center, Atlanta, Georgia.

James Brackett, B.A., Deputy Chief, Research Division, Office of Population, Technical Assistance Bureau, Agency for International Development, Washington, D.C.

Irvin M. Cushner, M.D., Associate Professor of Gynecology and Obstetrics, and Director, Center for Social Studies in Human Reproduction, The Johns Hopkins University School of Medicine, Baltimore, Maryland.

Henry P. David, Ph.D., Director of Research, International Research Institute, American Institutes for Research, Washington, D.C.

Emily C. Moore, M.A., M.S., Staff Associate, Demographic Division, The Population Council, New York, N. Y.

Charlotte Muller, Ph.D., Professor, Center for Social Research, City University of New York, New York, N. Y.

Edward Pohlman, Ph.D., Professor of Educational and Counseling Psychology, University of the Pacific, Stockton, California.

Nancy F. Russo, Ph.D., Associate Research Scientist, International Research Institute, American Institutes for Research, Washinghon, D.C.

Christopher Tietze, M.D., Associate Director, Bio-Medical Division, The Population Council, New York, N. Y.

Carl Tyler, M.D., Chief, Family Planning Evaluation Activity, Epidemiology Program, National Communicable Disease Center, Atlanta, Georgia.

Sanford R. Wolf, M.D., formerly Department of Psychiatry and Center for Social Studies in Human Reproduction, The Johns Hopkins University School of Medicine, Baltimore, Maryland; presently Assistant Professor and Director of Division of Liaison Psychiatry, Department of Psychiatry, School of Medicine, University of California, San Diego, La Jolla, California.

**Commentators:**

Robert E. Hall, M.D., Associate Professor of Clinical Obstetrics and Gynecology, College of Physicians and Surgeons, Columbia University, New York, N. Y.

Robert E. Markush, M.D., Chief, Center for Epidemiologic Studies, National Institute of Mental Health, Chevy Chase, Maryland.

Mindel Sheps, M.D., Professor of Biostatistics, School of Public Health, University of North Carolina, Chapel Hill, North Carolina.

**Observers:**

Eugene B. Brody, M.D., Professor of Psychiatry, and Head, Department of Psychiatry, University of Maryland School of Medicine, Baltimore, Maryland.

Philip Corfman, M.D., Director, Center for Population Research, National Institute of Child Health and Human Development, Bethesda, Maryland.

Zdenek Dytrych, M.D., Psychiatric Research Institute, Prague, Czechoslovakia.

Patricia Gabbett, B.S., Information Specialist, Office of Public Information, National Institute of Child Health and Human Developement, Bethesda, Maryland.

Donald Harting, M.D., Director, Family Planning Project, American Public Health Association, Washington, D.C.

Sarah Lewit, B.A., Research Associate, The Population Council, New York, N. Y.

Deborah Matory, M.S., Research Associate, National Medical Association Foundation, Inc., Washington, D.C.

Daniel Seigel, Sc.D., Statistician, Epidemiology and Biometry Branch,

National Institute of Child Health and Human Development, Bethesda, Maryland.

Donald E. Widmann, M.D., Assistant Professor of Psychiatry, Department of Psychiatry, North Carolina Memorial Hospital, University of North Carolina, Chapel Hill, North Carolina.

**Conference Staff:**

Betty Barton, M.S.W., Chief, Scientific Conference Branch, National Institute of Child Health and Human Development, Bethesda, Maryland.

Meryom Lebowitz, B.A., Conference Assistant, National Institute of Child Health and Human Development, Bethesda, Maryland.

# Index

Abortifacient drug: development of, 31
effect of, 152
Abortion: acceptance of, reasons for, 97
access to, effect of, 137
attempts, results of unsuccessful, 60
attitudes towards, 46–47, 63–65, 148
availability, use determined by, 135
complications of, 7, 8, 16, 24–30
contraceptives, interrelationship, 90, 110, 131, 134–148 *passim*
costs of, 92–93, 148–149, 177
criminal, 37, 51
decision to have, 75
denied, 69–70, 77, 110
desired, reporting difficulties, 70–71
economics of, 133, 165–166
facilities for, 92–93
groupings among those requesting, 65–66
illegal, mortality and morbidity in, 11–12
induced, 2, 8
information about, need for, 2
laws, 110, 139–140, 158
legal, 111, 165
legislation, effect on society's mores, 65
medical sequelae, research needs, 149–150
methods of, 11, 31–32, 188
nontherapeutic, complications of, 120–124 *passim*
performers of, 21
rate, 90, 137–138
ratios, 137–138, 158
research questions about, 35, 92, 93, 103, 109–111, 146–152, 187–192 *passim*
restricted, effect of, 165–167
restrictions, reasons for, 97
right, as a, 91
socio-economic factors, 192

socio-economic status, effect of, 117–118
spontaneous, 102
statistics, need for uniform, 37, 38, 39
surveillance program, 118–125
therapeutic, 45
use of, reasons for, 132–133
workshop concerning, 1–3
Adoption, 172
Albania, 82, 89
*American Journal of Public Health,* 1
Anaerobic organisms, 8
Anesthesia, complications of, 8
Anthropologist, role of, 150–151
Antizygotic drug, as abortifacient drug, 32
Armijo, R., 141, 143, 145

Beck, M. B., 72
Behavior disorders, 174
Belgrade, Yugoslavia, effect of family planning programs, 141
Birth control: abortion as, 91, 126, 128, 145
controversy over, 47
rejection of, 162
*See also* Contraception
Births: out-of-wedlock, 171
unwanted, number of, 173
Birth rates: correlation with abortion, 88
in countries of central and eastern Europe, 83, 84, 86–87, 103
in early marriage, 168
effect of abortion on, 104, 144
effect of age-sex structure on, 104
*See also* Czechoslovakia, Japan, Hungary, Poland, Yugoslavia, Soviet Union, Chile
Birth order, and unwanted children, 172

197